**ADVANCED SUBSIDIARY**

C000319758

# Revise AS
# General Studies

**Authors**

**Andy Collins**

**and**

**Martyn Groucutt**

# Contents

# Contents

# Specification lists

## AQA A General Studies

| MODULE | SPECIFICATION TOPIC | CHAPTER REFERENCE | STUDIED IN CLASS | REVISED | PRACTICE QUESTIONS |
|---|---|---|---|---|---|
| **Module 1 (M1)** Culture, morality, arts and humanities | Beliefs, values and moral reasoning | 5.1, 9.1, 9.2 | | | |
| | Religious belief and experience | 5.1 | | | |
| | The nature and importance of culture | 4.1, 4.2 | | | |
| | Creativity and innovation | 6.1, 6.2 | | | |
| | Aesthetic evaluation | 4.2 | | | |
| | Media and communication | 7.1, 7.2 | | | |
| **Module 2 (M2)** Science, mathematics and technology | Characteristics of the sciences | 8.1, 8.2 | | | |
| | Scientific objectivity and the question of progress | 8.1 | | | |
| | Scientific methods, principles, criteria | 8.1 | | | |
| | Social, ethical and environmental implications | 9.1, 9.2, 9.3 | | | |
| | Technology, science, culture and ideology | 10.1, 10.2 | | | |
| | Mathematical reasoning and application | 11.1, 11.2 | | | |
| **Module 3 (M3)** (with coursework option) Society, politics and the economy | Ideologies and values in society | 1.1, 1.2, 1.3, 5.1, 10.2 | | | |
| | Political processes and goals | 2.1, 2.2, 2.3, 2.4 | | | |
| | Objectivity in social science | 1.4 | | | |
| | Law, culture and ethics | 2.4 | | | |
| | Social and economic trends and constraints | 3.1, 3.2, 3.3 | | | |

## Examination analysis

The specification comprises three unit tests.

| | | | |
|---|---|---|---|
| **Unit 1** | Structured questions: multiple choice and a written task | 1hr 15 min test | 33.3% |
| **Unit 2** | Structured questions: multiple choice – mathematical and written | 1hr 15 min test | 33.3% |
| **Unit 3** Either: or: | Structured questions: extended writing assignment Coursework assignment | 1hr 15 min test | 33.3% |

# AQA B General Studies

| MODULE | SPECIFICATION TOPIC | CHAPTER REFERENCE | STUDIED IN CLASS | REVISED | PRACTICE QUESTIONS |
|---|---|---|---|---|---|
| **Module 1 (M1)** Conflict | Aggression | 1.1, 1.9 | | | |
| | Scientific controversy | 8.1, 8.2, 9.1, 9.2, 10.1, 10.2 | | | |
| | Social tension | 1.1, 1.2 | | | |
| | Popular and performing arts | 6.1, 7.1, 7.2 | | | |
| | Market forces | 3.1, 3.4 | | | |
| **Module 2 (M2)** Power | Stereotyping and stake-holdings | 1.1, 1.2, 1.3, 2.1, 4.1, 4.2, 5.1 | | | |
| | Fuels | 9.1, 9.2, 9.3 | | | |
| | Education and voting | 1.2, 1.3 | | | |
| | Media influence | 7.1, 7.2 | | | |
| | Advertising and globalisation | 1.3, 7.2 | | | |
| | Powers – social and religious | 2.1, 2.2, 2.3, 2.4, 5.1, 5.2 | | | |
| **Module 3 (M3)** Space | Mathematical reasoning and its application | 11.1, 11.2 | | | |
| | Climate change | 9.2, 9.3 | | | |
| | Housing and migration | 1.2, 3.1, 3.3 | | | |
| | 3-D art and global media | 4.1, 6.2, 7.1, 7.2 | | | |
| | Land use and access | 3.3, 9.3 | | | |
| | Environmental | 9.1, 9.3, 10.2 | | | |

## Examination analysis

The specification comprises three unit tests.

| **Unit 1** | Structured questions: extended paragraph answers | 1hr 15 min test | 33.3% |
|---|---|---|---|
| **Unit 2** | Structured questions: one written task, one extended essay | 1hr 15 min test | 33.3% |
| **Unit 3** | Structured questions: data response | 1hr 15 min test | 33.3% |

## Edexcel General Studies

| MODULE | SPECIFICATION TOPIC | CHAPTER REFERENCE | STUDIED IN CLASS | REVISED | PRACTICE QUESTIONS |
|---|---|---|---|---|---|
| **Module 1 (M1)** Aspects of culture | Understanding and appreciation of the nature and importance of culture | 4.1 | | | |
| | Beliefs, values and moral reasoning | 5.1, 9.1, 9.2 | | | |
| | Religious belief and experience | 5.1 | | | |
| | Creativity and innovation | 6.1, 6.2 | | | |
| | Aesthetic evaluation | 4.2 | | | |
| | Media and communication | 7.1, 7.2 | | | |
| **Module 2 (M2)** Scientific horizons | Characteristics of the sciences | 8.1, 8.2 | | | |
| | The nature of scientific objectivity, and the question of progress | 8.1 | | | |
| | Scientific methods, principles and criteria | 8.1 | | | |
| | Social, ethical and environmental implications of discoveries and developments | 9.1, 9.2, 9.3 | | | |
| | Mathematical reasoning and its application | 11.1, 11.2 | | | |
| | The relationship between technology, science, culture and ideology | 10.1, 10.2 | | | |
| **Module 3 (M3)** Social perspectives (with coursework option) | Ideologies and values in society | 1.1, 1.2, 1.3, 5.1, 10.2 | | | |
| | Political processes and goals | 2.1, 2.2, 2.3, 2.4 | | | |
| | Objectivity in social sciences, explanation and evaluation of human behaviour | 1.1, 1.2, 1.3, 1.4 | | | |

## Examination analysis

The specification comprises three unit tests.

| | | | |
|---|---|---|---|
| **Unit 1** | Structured questions: short and extended answers, stimulus material | 1hr 30 min test | 40% |
| **Unit 2** | Structured questions: short and extended answers, stimulus material | 1hr 15 min test | 30% |
| **Unit 3** Either: or: | Structured questions: short and extended answers (include.mathematical reasoning), stimulus material Coursework assignment | 1hr 30 min test | 30% |

# OCR General Studies

| MODULE | SPECIFICATION TOPIC | CHAPTER REFERENCE | STUDIED IN CLASS | REVISED | PRACTICE QUESTIONS |
|---|---|---|---|---|---|
| **Module 1 (M1)** <br> *The cultural domain* | *Beliefs, values and moral reasoning* | *5.1, 9.1, 9.2* | | | |
| | *Aspects of culture* | *4.1, 4.2, 6.1, 6.2, 10.1* | | | |
| | *Media and communication* | *7.1, 7.2* | | | |
| **Module 2 (M2)** <br> *The scientific domain (with coursework option)* | *Characteristics of the sciences* | *8.1, 8.2, 10.1, 10.2* | | | |
| | *Scientific method, principles, criteria* | *8.1, 9.1, 9.2* | | | |
| | *Mathematical reasoning and application* | *11. 1, 11.2* | | | |
| **Module 3 (M3)** <br> *The social domain* | *Political systems, processes and goals* | *2.1, 2.2, 2.3* | | | |
| | *Objectivity in social science* | *1.4* | | | |
| | *Social and economic constraints* | *1.1, 1.2, 1.3, 3.1, 3.2, 3.3* | | | |

## Examination analysis

The specification comprises three unit tests.

| | | | |
|---|---|---|---|
| **Unit 1** | Structured questions: multiple choice and a written task | *1hr 15 min test* | *33.3%* |
| **Unit 2** | Structured questions: multiple choice – mathematical and written | *1hr 15 min test* | *33.3%* |
| **Unit 3** <br> Either: <br> or: | Structured questions: extended writing assignment <br> Coursework assignment | *1hr 15 min test* | *33.3%* |

# AS/A2 Level General Studies courses

## AS and A2

All General Studies A Level courses being studied from September 2000 are in two parts, with three separate modules in each part. Students first study the AS (Advanced Subsidiary) course. Some will then go on to study the second part of the A Level course, called A2. Advanced Subsidiary is assessed at the standard expected halfway through an A Level course: i.e., between GCSE and Advanced GCE. This means that new AS and A2 courses are designed so that difficulty steadily increases:

• A2 General Studies builds from AS General Studies.

## How will you be tested?

### Assessment units

For AS General Studies, you will be tested by three assessment units. For the full A Level in General Studies, you will take a further three units. AS General Studies forms 50% of the assessment weighting for the full A Level.

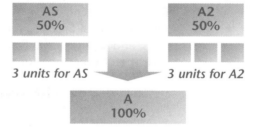

Each unit can normally be taken in either January or June, except for the sixth, which has to be taken at the end. Alternatively, you can study the whole course before taking any of the unit tests. There is a lot of flexibility about when exams can be taken and the diagram below shows just some of the ways that the assessment units may be taken for AS and A Level General Studies.

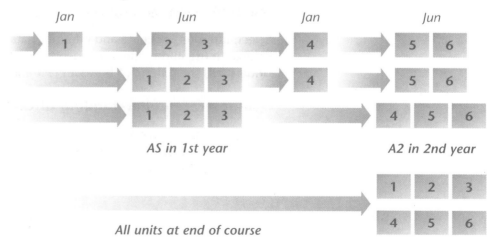

If you are disappointed with a module result, you can resit each module once. You will need to be very careful about when you take up a resit opportunity because you will have only one chance to improve your mark. The higher mark counts.

### A2 and Synoptic assessment

After having studied AS General Studies, you may wish to continue studying General Studies to A Level. For this you will need to take three further units of General Studies at A2. Similar assessment arrangements apply except for the final unit, that draws together different parts of the course in a synoptic assessment and has to be assessed at the end of the course.

### Coursework

Coursework may form part of your AS or A2 General Studies course depending on the specification. However, it is optional in all specifications.

### Key skills

It is important that you develop your key skills throughout your AS and A2 courses. These are important skills that you need whatever you do beyond AS and A Levels. To gain the key skills qualification you will need to collect evidence together in a 'portfolio' to show that you have attained Level 3 in Communication, Application of number and Information technology. You will also need to take a formal testing in each key skill. You will have many opportunities during AS General Studies to develop your key skills.

It is a worthwhile qualification, as it demonstrates your ability to put your ideas across to other people, collect data and use up-to-date technology in your work.

## What skills will I need?

For AS General Studies, you will be tested by assessment objectives: these are the skills and abilities that you should have acquired by studying the course. The assessment objectives for AS General Studies are shown below.

### Knowledge with understanding

- Skills gained from different disciplines

### Communicate clearly

- Quality of language
- Able to use language in a concise, logical and relevant way

### Marshal evidence and draw conclusions

- Select, interpret, evaluate and interpret data and written information
- Be able to use information provided to develop arguments
- Understand the difference between fact and assertion

### Demonstrate understanding of different types of knowledge

- Show an understanding of different types of knowledge
- Be able to see the relationship between them
- Be able to appreciate their limitations

# Different types of questions in AS examinations

In AS General Studies examinations, different types of questions are used to assess your abilities and skills. There are also some differences in the types of questions set in the different examinations.

## Short-answer questions

These take the form of asking you to analyse and respond to short pieces of stimulus material (for example, a newspaper headline, some data or an advert). This can be either a written or a data-response answer. They are found in the AQA specifications A and B, and the Edexcel and OCR specifications.

## Multiple choice objective questions

These take the form of questions with several possible answers and you have to choose which one is correct. Such questions feature in the AQA specification A and Edexcel papers.

## Extended writing

This takes two main forms:

(i) the traditional essay written in response to a question
(ii) the creation of an argument to put forward based on stimulus material provided with the paper.

All of the specifications use both types of extended writing to some extent. The quality of your writing forms part of the assessment, as does your ability to examine a variety of sources and use them efficiently.

# Four steps to successful revision

## Step 1: Understand

- Study the topic to be learned slowly. Make sure you understand the logic or important concepts
- Mark up the text if necessary – underline, highlight and make notes
- Re-read each paragraph slowly.

**GO TO STEP 2**

## Step 2: Summarise

- Now make your own revision note summary:
  What is the main idea, theme or concept to be learned?
  What are the main points? How does the logic develop?
  Ask questions: Why? How? What next?
- Use bullet points, mind maps, patterned notes
- Link ideas with mnemonics, mind maps, crazy stories
- Note the title and date of the revision notes
  (e.g. General Studies: Social class, 3rd March)
- Organise your notes carefully and keep them in a file.

**This is now in short term memory. You will forget 80% of it if you do not go to Step 3.
GO TO STEP 3, but first take a 10 minute break.**

## Step 3: Memorise

- Take 25 minute learning 'bites' with 5 minute breaks
- After each 5 minute break test yourself:
  Cover the original revision note summary
  Write down the main points
  Speak out loud (record on tape)
  Tell someone else
  Repeat many times.

**The material is well on its way to long term memory.
You will forget 40% if you do not do step 4. GO TO STEP 4**

## Step 4: Track/Review

- Create a Revision Diary (one A4 page per day)
- Make a revision plan for the topic, e.g. 1 day later, 1 week later, 1 month later.
- Record your revision in your Revision Diary, e.g.
  General Studies: Social class, 3rd March 25 minutes
  General Studies: Social class, 5th March 15 minutes
  General Studies: Social class, 3rd April 15 minutes
  ... and then at monthly intervals.

# Chapter 1
# Society

**The following topics are covered in this chapter:**

- *The family*
- *Social class*

- *Education*
- *Objectivity in social sciences*

## 1.1 The family

*After studying this section you should be able to:*

- *identify the range of family types*
- *describe changes to the family – particularly since 1945*
- *explain gender, marriage and divorce issues*

LEARNING SUMMARY

### Family structures

AQA A   M3
AQA B   M1
EDEXCEL   M3

The vast majority of people in the UK have been brought up in families. However, as you probably realise, there is a great variety of family structures within today's society – a view highlighted by the differing types of family life found in popular television programmes.

There is the conventional family: husband, wife and children (it may be worth considering why the word 'conventional' is used); the one-parent family; the inter-generational family; and couples who live together outside marriage. All these are easily recognisable in a 'soap' such as *Eastenders*.

The recent decision (in September 1999) by OXO to drop its long-running 'family' commercial, operational since 1983, also indicates that there may be changes occurring to the concept of the 'conventional' family.

> A nuclear family means one based on the unit of mother, father and children.

In this century we have become accustomed to the concept of the **nuclear family**. As long ago as 1949, the social anthropologist Murdoch defined the family as:

> A social group characterised by common residence, economic co-operation and reproduction. It includes adults of both sexes, at least two of whom maintain a socially approved sexual relationship and one or more children, own or adopted, of the sexually cohabiting adults.
>
> *Murdoch 1949*

Murdoch argued that this family unit performed four functions:

- it 'controls' sexual behaviour
- it produces the next generation for society

- it acts as a basic economic unit
- it socialises children into their roles in their society.

> An extended family is one that includes more than three generations living under the same roof.

The other major group of family life is the **extended family**. Arguably, before the introduction of the Welfare State in the first half of the twentieth century, the extended family was essential because it helped in such areas as **accommodation**, **sickness**, **unemployment** and **old age**.

If this is true and if the Welfare State is supposed to protect us 'from cradle to grave', have extended families ceased to exist? If so, why? If not, why not?

### Family life today and change

AQA A   M3
AQA B   M1
EDEXCEL   M3

The overriding view of the family, popularised by advertisers and politicians alike, is that of the nuclear family. (Leading politicians of all parties try to conjure up a rose-tinted view of the family by demanding a return to 'family values'). This image of the typical family is misleading. In 1992 less than 25 per cent of the households in the UK consisted of a married couple and one or more dependent children. As

There are at least four reasons why extended families still exist:

- Many ethnic groups live in extended family situations.
- Grandparents can be very useful as baby-sitters or child-minders if both parents work.
- Extended families can keep in touch much more easily because of improved communications.
- Geography is no longer such a problem so the extended family can provide support for family members in times of need or crisis.

with all statistics, however, this could be misleading. It may be preferable to consider what could be called a person's 'family life-cycle':

- birth, childhood
- single adulthood
- marriage/cohabitation
- parenthood
- middle age – children leaving home
- old age.

For some of the elements of this cycle it is probable that a person will be part of a nuclear family, for others he or she will not. (You should be able to identify examples of each.)

Some of the changes in family life are related to alterations in the structure of life itself in the UK.

- **Divorce** – the increasing ease with which divorce is attainable. The 1969 Divorce Act, allowing divorce on the grounds of 'irretrievable breakdown of a marriage' has inevitably led to far more one-parent families. In 1972 there were 650,000 lone parent families in the UK. By 1992 that figure had doubled. This represents 20 per cent of all families with dependent children.

- **Increasing life expectancy** – we are living longer. A larger proportion of people survive into old age and, hence, many households comprise single people or married couples only. As women generally live longer than men, many single-person households are made up of elderly widows.

- **Greater personal control** – now that contraception is freely available, abortion is generally obtainable and society has grown to accept the concept of single-parent families and unmarried mothers, there has been a change in social mores. However, society still aims for both partners to make valid contributions to the lives of children. The introduction of the Child Support Agency in 1993, with the aim of tracking down absent fathers and forcing them to provide financial support, has not been a resounding success. It does, however, reflect the ambivalent attitude towards single-parent families present in our society.

## Remarriage and reconstituted families

The 1991 General Household Survey showed that 80 per cent of men and 75 per cent of women who divorce before the age of 35 remarry within ten years. It is these new families – which, quite possibly have children from previous marriages or relationships (and may wish to have children in the new relationship) – that can be called 'reconstituted' families and they represent an increasing phenomenon in the UK. Approximately six million people live in such families – families where pressures such as negotiations with natural parents over access, holidays, etc. can cause problems. Such difficulties could be a reason for the fact that the divorce rate amongst the already divorced is much higher than among those in their first marriage.

> There are four main groupings of the family unit: nuclear; extended; single-parent and reconstituted families.  **KEY POINT**

## Gender, marriage and divorce

AQA A  M3
AQA B  M1
EDEXCEL  M3

### Gender roles

The roles of men and women inside the family have changed dramatically since 1945. Some of the reasons for these changes are demographic:

**Family size** – this has decreased since World War II. The average number of children in a family is now less than two.

**Marriage** – although increasingly popular until the early 1970s (these were the offspring of the 'baby boom' era at the end of World War II), the trend has now reversed and a large proportion of couples are now not getting married.

**Life expectancy** – a longer life means that many couples now contemplate the wife returning to full-time employment after rearing children – if, indeed, she stopped work at all.

By the early 1990s, two-thirds of married women were employed outside the home. Although statistically women earn less than men, women's earnings make an important contribution to family income.

The equality movement for women in the 1960s and 1970s has had significant results, particularly in the field of employment. The realisation that women had far more economic power than had been appreciated has been the reason in part for technological improvements that save time and effort in the home:

- microwave ovens – assisting rapid meal preparation
- automatic washing machines
- duvets
- central heating systems ... and so on.

The other spin-off relating to women's economic independence through work is the sharing of tasks inside the home between husband and wife. Preparation of evening meals, shopping, organisation of household bills and household repairs are increasingly shared between couples. However, various sociologists, such as Edgell (1980) have shown that decisions about who does what are based on whether it is a 'serious' task or not (i.e. perhaps the male has a greater say with regard to decisions such as moving house).

## Marriage and alternatives

Marriage and its popularity is in decline: in 1971 459,000 marriages took place; in 1991 there were 350,000 marriages. In the same period the number of divorces doubled. On the other hand, cohabitation (i.e. living together outside marriage) has increased. Between 1979 and 1991 the proportion of married women cohabiting rose from 11 per cent to 23 per cent. In 1971, 8 per cent of births were outside marriage; in 1991 this had risen to 31 per cent.

There are several reasons put forward to explain these statistics:

- cohabitation could be seen as a prelude to marriage
- marriage can be seen as unnecessary
- some women and men want children but not necessarily to make a formal commitment to each other
- the financial costs of the wedding ceremony and reception.

## Divorce

This has greatly increased in the twentieth century. This may prove that marriage is in terminal decline, or simply that families have a more open and honest approach to each other. The increase in divorce has not been consistent. There was a large increase after 1945 because of upheavals caused by World War II.

The 1960s saw a steady rise in the rate of divorce and once the Divorce Reform Act came into effect in 1971 there was a greater increase. (However, since 1980 the divorce rate appears to have stabilised.)There were several reasons for this increase:

**Removal of legal and financial constraints** – Before 1857 an Act of Parliament was needed for a divorce to be granted, consequently it happened rarely. Until 1923 adultery was the main grounds for divorce, and in 1937 this was extended to include insanity, desertion and cruelty. The 1948 Legal Aid Act was crucial in providing financial help to those who wanted to get divorced. In 1971, the Act allowed for 'irretrievable breakdown of marriage'. This meant that couples could divorce after two years' separation by mutual consent or five years if one of them objected. An Act of Parliament in 1984 reduced the time limit for divorce from a minimum of three years of marriage to one year.

**Changed expectations of family life** – People began to have expectations of being happy within marriage – if that did not happen, with the opportunities to divorce now becoming available, they would end the marriage.

**Changes to women's social position** – 75 per cent of divorce petitions are made by women. Increased financial independence means that they can now opt out of marriages within which they are unhappy.

**Changing social values** – The stigma attached to divorce have now disappeared in most circles – royal divorces emphasise this. Couples also stay together less often 'for the sake of the children'.

**Demographic changes** – Arguably marriages at an early age in the 1960s and 1970s have meant the possibility of very long marriages. This could itself be a contributory factor towards the divorce rate. By the 1980s couples possibly lived together before marriage – hence marrying later.

## Progress check

**1** Why are there fewer children per family?

**2** Why does divorce happen more frequently?

1 Contraception; lower infant mortality; cost of children; both partners working.
2 Easier to obtain; marriage is less likely to be seen as a life-time commitment; increased expectations of married life.

# 1.2 Social class

*After studying this section you should be able to:*

- *identify the components that contribute towards class*
- *explain the concept of social mobility*

LEARNING SUMMARY

## What is 'class'?

| AQA A | M3 |
| AQA B | M1 |
| EDEXCEL | M3 |
| OCR | M3 |

We need to start by establishing what exactly is social class.

- Sociologists normally refer to 'social strata' rather than social class. 'Social stratification' means the social divisions that appear in any society. There is no one distinctive list of the varying strata as these vary from age to age – for example, the feudal system in Medieval England, or its equivalent inside France, which was a contributory factor to the French Revolution. Today, in places such as India, the caste system, although illegal, still operates in practice. This means there is a very strict demarcation line between groups, making movement very difficult.

- Definition of social class can be quite narrow. In other words, social class can be deduced by income, property or occupation. Wider definitions try to take on board the fact that groupings develop similar social and cultural characteristics.

All of the examination board specifications cover this concept and it is important to have some clear views relating to social class. Vague generalisations do not get you very far in answering examination questions!

> Social stratification exists in all cultures and means that a society possesses a way of dividing social groups within that society.
>
> KEY POINT

Division into groups or strata can be quite difficult and the groupings vary. For example, the 1991 Census divided people into:

1 professional
2 managerial/technical
3 skilled non-manual/skilled manual
4 partly skilled
5 unskilled.

The basis for the above groupings is *occupation* – as is the breakdown in the Registrar General's Social Class Scheme:

1 professional
2 intermediate
3 skilled non-manual
4 skilled manual
5 semi-skilled
6 unskilled manual.

It would therefore seem that occupation is a major criterion of social class. But how do people get their occupations? Nowadays. **education and qualifications** are essential pre-requisites for various occupations. Moving that debate further forward – does the type of school you go to matter? Or the college of higher education? Or the university? In other words, are you likely (whatever the qualifications you achieve) to obtain a better class of occupation if you went to Mob Lane secondary school, or King Edward VIII Grammar School, or Wandsworth University or Oxbridge University?

Occupation and educational qualifications can be seen as important elements of class. Overall, **income** can also have a vital bearing. Possibly, however, it may be necessary to investigate whether the income is inherited or obtained. In other words, is Liam Gallagher in the same class as the Duke of Devonshire? Palpably not – yet possibly their income is similar. So, as mentioned earlier, beware of vague generalisations: 'if you're rich you must be upper class' is not valid – it can be on occasions, but not generally.

Possibly another tool to be used in assessing class could be that of **power**. If someone has a large element of power (e.g. a headteacher) are they in a higher class than the pupils and staff over whom they have the power? Again the answer is: possibly! It is very difficult to be categorical in issues relating to class.

No matter how hard it may be to analyse the components of class, in addition to occupation, income and power, there are certain other undeniable concepts.

### Housing
In 1993 90 per cent of professional households were owner occupied (compared with 42 per cent of unskilled manual). This was despite the Thatcherite revolution that allowed council house tenants to buy their properties.

### Life expectancy
As a generalisation, those who live in the most affluent communities can expect to live up to eight years longer than those in deprived areas.

### Social habits
In 1992 people in the unskilled manual group were three times more likely to smoke than those in the professional group.

### Education
Far fewer entrants to British universities were from the unskilled class compared with the top two classes.

## Progress check

For each of the four points above, give three reasons why you think these statistics are so.

Remember, good answers always begin with a plan.

You may have suggested:
- **Housing:** professionals have regular salaries; it is easier for professionals to get mortgages; unskilled people are not willing to take on the responsibilities of house ownership; many professionals have inherited wealth which makes it easier to become an owner occupier.
- **Life expectancy:** private health schemes; better health education; better living conditions; better quality food, etc.
- **Social habits:** less knowledge of dangers; as more of their colleagues smoke it becomes a self-fulfilling prophecy; their jobs are more boring; the habit is passed down from generation to generation.
- **Education:** increased cost, and erosion of grant system; value put on higher education; most unskilled class leave school at the earliest opportunity.

## Social mobility

| | |
|---|---|
| AQA A | M3 |
| AQA B | M1 |
| EDEXCEL | M3 |
| OCR | M3 |

Social mobility means that people can move across strata from one level to another. In the last few decades, opportunities for mobility have increased inside the UK. There are various reasons for this.

### Education
The increasing availability of further and higher education, the increase in volume of universities, etc. have meant that a greater proportion of the population can obtain graduate qualifications. You will be aware of the year-on-year increase in the numbers sitting A Levels. Increased qualifications opens doors to occupations that were previously closed.

### Occupations themselves have changed
With the advent of computerisation there is a greater demand for non-manual skills and less for manual skills – e.g. the decline of the craft apprenticeship. This is also emphasised by the shift from 'blue collar' workers towards the mainly service 'white collar' workers sector.

### Old school tie network and 'connections' still exist
For example, knowing the right people, being in the right club, etc. can be an agent for social mobility. However, some would argue that educational qualifications are now a greater facilitator of social mobility, e.g. as a result of having gone to a particular university.

### Media and entertainment stars
Stars can use their power and influence to move socially upwards. For example, Elton John on almost all criteria was working class, but his successes have ensured that no social doors are now closed to him. The same can be said for major television personalities, e.g. Chris Evans, or famous sports stars, e.g. Linford Christie. It would be interesting to analyse whether this kind of social mobility is maintained by people in this category once their 'star has waned'. (For example, does George Best enjoy the same social mobility that he had twenty-five years ago?)

> Social mobility can be upwards, e.g. a roadsweeper's son who qualifies as a lawyer, or downwards, e.g. a lawyer's son who becomes a bus driver.

> Social mobility is the obvious difference between the class system and the caste system where no movement is allowed. In other words, the position in the caste strata system is ascribed, i.e. fixed at birth. Our system places more emphasis on achievement, i.e. what people can do.

**KEY POINT**

Social mobility means that people can move within the levels of social stratification in the society of which they are a part.

## The underclass

> This means the disadvantaged and marginalised group at the 'bottom' of society.

On the surface there appears to be a general moving up of social class (i.e. even poor families can afford basic technical items such as washing machines, fridges, etc.). Linked to this, the progressive tax system (mentioned later) also ensures a levelling out of the different classes. However, there is increasing concern about the development of an underclass.

**KEY POINT**

Where there is an underclass in society it means, in effect, that there is a group that is excluded from the general prosperity of the population.

The main reasons leading to the development of an underclass are as follows.

### Economic
These people are deprived and impoverished because of:
- a lack of employment
- declining levels of employment
- changes in the nature of employment (e.g. part-time work, casual workforce)
- the rise in the number of one-parent families (900,000 in 1981 to 1,300,000 in 1991). Most one-parent families are led by females, likely to be paid little because of difficulties in finding adequate child-care

- the social security system has not been given adequate benefits to help people in this sector. This is a governmental decision, but successive governments have been urged on by electorates to fight against 'social-security scroungers', etc.

### Social factors
- the long-term unemployed
- one-parent families and
- elderly pensioners

all feeling alienated from society. In other words, perhaps the safety net of the Welfare State has not caught many of these groups.

### Cross-cultural features
There is a strong debate about this.

- Some social scientists claim the underclass are poor because of their values (e.g. laziness, lack of self-esteem) and take advantage of an over-generous welfare state.

- Others argue that governments persuade us that the problems of the underclass are their own fault – because the UK is a land of opportunity and people who do not seize opportunities must be viewed as failures. (It is possible here to compare these ideas with those that were found in Nazi Germany.)

- Others argue that the main reason for the existence of the underclass lies in the structural inequalities of society itself. In other words, the underclass share the same values as anyone else but their opportunities are severely restricted.

Whatever the validity of these points it is fairly clear that the longer people are part of the underclass, the more likely it is that they will stay there and thus become part of a self-fulfilling prophecy – accustomed to dependency and powerlessness and losing motivation and discipline to improve their living standards.

## The growth of the classless society

| AQA A | M3 |
| AQA B | M1 |
| EDEXCEL | M3 |
| OCR | M3 |

In the mid-1990s John Major's Conservative Government referred to 'the classless society', and there are arguments that we are moving in that direction. For example, equal opportunities on the surface appear to be a valid assumption. Everyone has the opportunity to make of themselves what they wish. Yet for some of the reasons indicated above, this does not always happen. At best, equal opportunities can be seen as providing certain opportunities for people in the lower social classes to become more socially mobile.

By 'levelling' is meant ways in which extremes in society, particularly in wealth, are moderated.

There has always been a large element of levelling in society, e.g.

- a progressive tax system which taxes the more wealthy
- the fact that as status symbols, e.g. cars, foreign holidays, become comparatively cheaper, then a greater proportion of people can access them.

However, despite these factors, elements of class are still with us.

## Progress check

Try to think of three reasons why social mobility is a good thing and three reasons why it is bad.

You may have suggested the following:

**Good:** it lets the 'best' and 'brightest' move upwards; it ensures that people not worthy of their position in society become less important; talent/power, etc. is recognised but is based on a person's ability not on inherited wealth, etc.

**Bad:** a run of bad luck can lead to a move down the social ladder; it leads to a lack of stability in society; why should the 'best' dominate our society – who says they are the best?

# 1.3 Education

After studying this section you should be able to:

- *describe the compulsory nature of education*
- *explain why there is a national curriculum*
- *analyse and discuss selection arguments*

LEARNING SUMMARY

## Formal education

| | |
|---|---|
| AQA A | M3 |
| AQA B | M1 |
| EDEXCEL | M3 |
| OCR | M3 |

Tony Blair's main priority on becoming prime minister was 'education, education, education'. By this he meant the formal stages of education from the statutory ages (i.e. 5–16), plus pre-school (i.e. nursery and play groups) as well as post-statutory (i.e. sixth form, sixth form college, further education college). He also probably had in mind the rapidly increasing university sector. It is doubtful, however, that he considered the informal education process that takes place as a result of socialisation.

Socialisation is the process by which we learn the culture of our society. It is a life-long process, but the early years of a person's life are the most important. This is when 'primary socialisation' takes place inside the aegis of the family.

Compulsory formal education is comparatively recent. The 1870 Education Act is usually seen as the landmark act that made schooling compulsory. However, as late as 1947–8 pupils could leave school aged 14 (Year 9). Enforcing a leaving age of 16 took place in 1973. An increasing percentage of pupils stay on past GCSE examinations in further or higher education.

### The structure of formal education in the UK

Education is divided into two main stages:

**Primary**
Usually for those aged 5 to 11. This can be further subdivided into:
- 5 to 7 (Infant)
- 7 to 11 (Junior)
- or straight through 5 to 11.

*NB* A few local education authorities still have Middle schools (i.e. 9–13, or 8–12) with infant/primary schools feeding into them.

**Secondary**
This is provided through the following:
- 11–16: comprehensive/grammar/secondary modern
- 11–18: comprehensive/grammar
- 16–18: sixth form college/further education college.

### The selection system

**Grammar:** intended for pupils seen as academic. Today there are only 160 grammar schools in the country.

**Technical:** intended for those with an aptitude for technical subjects.

**Secondary modern:** 75% of the population attended these. In many respects they taught a watered-down academic curriculum, but with far more emphasis on practical subjects such as woodwork, metalwork, and needlework.

Even in the heyday of grammar schools, after the 1944 Education Act had set up the so-called 'tri-partite' system i.e. grammar, technical and secondary modern schools, only 20 per cent of the population went to grammars. Pupils attending secondary modern schools were the 'hewers of wood and drawers of water'. In an era of large numbers of manual jobs, these pupils were thus given a basic education.

The problem with the system was that of selection. How do you choose the 'brighter' or 'academic' pupils? The answer was (and still is): by the 11+ examination.

> Grammar schools catered for the academically able top 20 per cent of the population; technical colleges were aimed at those who had an aptitude for technical subjects and secondary modern schools (for those less academic) accommodated 75 per cent of school pupils.

KEY POINT

The 11+, or scholarship test, followed on from the 1944 Act. Most grammar schools which use selection, use a format of 11+ examination. Many grammar schools are found in the south-east (e.g. Kent), Yorkshire, and in some inner-city areas, (e.g. Walsall).

Grant maintained schools were those where parents had voted to 'opt out' of local government control, so that the school was given more money from the government to provide services for itself and not expect the local authority to deliver these services.

## Comprehensive education

Generally in the past, the Labour Party has favoured comprehensive education and the Conservatives have held that an 'appropriate' education for everyone is necessary, which could be construed as support for grammar schools.

The majority of secondary schools in this country are now comprehensive, although since September 1999 they are officially called 'community schools'. The only exception to these are the former 'grant maintained' schools (set up under the last Conservative administration) which are now called 'foundation schools'.

Some of the original features about comprehensive schools (i.e. social mixing and mixed ability teaching) no longer really apply. Most comprehensive schools now 'set' or 'stream' their pupils. Whilst there are no longer rigorous catchment areas that define where pupils must go to school, many schools are seen as exclusively one class (i.e. middle or working class).

> Comprehensive education is based on the principle that every child should be able to be educated in the same educational establishment as other children in his neighbourhood irrespective of ability.

**KEY POINT**

## Progress check

Try and construct arguments both for and against the 11+ selection system.

You may have thought of the following:

**Arguments for the 11+**
It gives the country an elite of people with excellent brains who can run the country; it stretches the most able; it ensures that like-minded people can be kept socially isolated in order to make rapid progress.

**Arguments against the 11+**
Is a test at 11 an adequate way of dividing pupils according to ability? What about late developers? People who 'failed' the 11+ may feel second class and therefore perform as second class. What about people on the margin between failure and success at 11? Rich people could afford to have their children coached in order to succeed in the 11+; it divides children socially.

## The National Curriculum

| | |
|---|---|
| AQA A | M3 |
| AQA B | M1 |
| EDEXCEL | M3 |
| OCR | M3 |

### Schools as businesses

As we approached the millennium, schools became much more like businesses. The reason for this emanated from legislation laid down in the late 1980s. There were two prongs to the changes:

**The National Curriculum**
This was set up in 1988, dividing pupils into 'key stages' for learning:

- Key Stage 1: 5 – 7 years
- Key Stage 2: 7 – 11 years
- Key Stage 3: 11 – 14 years
- Key Stage 4: 14 – 16 years.

For the first time schools were told what subjects to teach and the content of those subjects, and this has led to increased centralisation of the education system. The formulation of tests at the end of each Key Stage (with KS4 being the GCSE hurdle) has opened the way for direct school-by-school comparison and the innovation of league tables. This, in itself, has led to increased competition and the labelling of schools as 'good' or 'bad'.

**Local management of schools**
The introduction of Local management of schools (LMS) means that schools control their own budget. This budget is to a large extent being decided by the number of pupils inside the school. In other words, every pupil has a price on his/her head. This has led to large amounts of marketing on the part of schools, with competition being very intense. Schools who face falling numbers on the roll (for whatever reason) then have to make cuts to balance the budget ... often meaning staff redundancy.

**KEY POINT**

Local management of schools (LMS) means that all schools have to manage their own budget.

> There are schools which charge fees for some or all pupils. They form the private sector of education.

### Private Education

There are about 2,000 independent schools across the UK. In 1991, 7 per cent of all pupils attended independent schools and by the age of 16, 18 per cent of boys and 15 per cent of girls attended these schools. Most of the pupils who attend independent schools are from an upper-class background. There are obviously arguments both for and against private education.

*For:*
- People should have the right to choose their children's education.
- Parents should have the right to use their money for whatever they want.
- Parents believe that private education gives their children a better start in life.
- Academically, independent schools often obtain better results.
- Superior facilities and smaller class sizes are available.

*Against:*
- It gives some people an advantage over others, in areas such as smaller classes (which usually lead to better academic results) and in terms of 'old school tie' networks that can facilitate university entry, etc.
- It perpetrates a class-ridden system.
- The overall cost of these institutions would be better utilised in a total state structure where there would be economies of scale.

# 1.4 Objectivity in the social sciences

*After studying this section you should be able to:*

- *distinguish between facts and opinions*
- *understand the differences between natural and social sciences*

**LEARNING SUMMARY**

## The nature of social science

| | |
|---|---|
| AQA A | M3 |
| AQA B | M1 |
| EDEXCEL | M3 |
| OCR | M3 |

> Natural science means areas such as Physics, Chemistry, Biology, where pure cause and effect can be studied and comprehended.

You may have found so far in this chapter that for many of the questions that you have been asked to consider there is not necessarily a totally correct answer. The main reason for this is that social science is not an exact science, in the way that a natural science (such as Biology) is. The latter relies on pure, unalterable facts; the former, although it has some theories associated with it, does not have exclusive answers.

We can start by thinking about ourselves and how we make decisions. Are they completely our own choice or are they shaped by factors in society that impinge on us? In other words, are decisions made by 'free will' or are they 'determined'? Clearly, these two concepts are not mutually exclusive, but rather a matter of emphasis between two sides.

Groups of people who think about the power of society over the individuals refer to 'social systems'. They argue that these systems make and control the individuals inside society – so people are what they are because of the pressures and expectations put upon them.

The counter-argument to this is that individuals have the ability to exert control over their own actions. In other words, society is what the individuals inside it, make it!

Free will is where the individual exercises personal choice in decision-making. Determinism is where other factors (such as society) exert more power.

## Progress check

If you are assuming that after A Levels you may consider moving on to higher education, what factors would be the main ones in making your decision? How many of these would fall into 'free will' and how many into 'determinism'?

Factors you could consider might be:
(a) a desire to go to University;
(b) obtaining good grades at A Level;
(c) the need for a student loan;
(d) the cost of leaving home;
(e) a wish to stay in the local area.
Examples of determinism are (b) and (d).

### Sociology as a science

Sociology is often referred to as a social science because early sociologists were convinced that the following of scientific methods would enable them to discover the laws underlying the development of human society.

Auguste Comte (1798–1857) believed that sociology based on natural-science methodology would result in a 'positive science of sociology' or 'Positivism'. Only directly observable facts were acceptable as evidence and these facts needed to be put into numerical form. Today, positivism is often used to describe a range of approaches that reflect the methods and assumptions of the natural sciences – including those of Emile Durkheim (1858–1917) and Karl Popper (1902–).

Emile Durkheim in his *Rules of Sociological Method* (1895) argued: 'Consider social facts as things – so they can be treated in the same way as the objects, events and processes of the natural world.' However, there are problems with Comte and Durkheim's view:

- Because they have consciousness, humans are totally different from the inanimate objects that make up the natural world.
- It is therefore very difficult to use natural-science methods to study human behaviour.

Durkheim argued that theories should come from evidence – the evidence would produce the theories. This is known as the 'inductive approach'.

The inductive approach to sociology is where evidence produces the theories.

The reverse of this is the 'deductive approach' – in other words, we start with a theory and use information to test the theory. This approach was followed by Karl Popper, who believed that theories could be tested and found to be falsified (i.e. proved wrong). However, even theories that survive falsification tests need not be true. The famous example of 'All swans are white' is a scientific statement because it can be falsified.

The statement 'All swans are white' is only true or valid until the first non-white swan is seen. At that point it becomes fatally flawed!

The deductive approach to sociology is to formulate a theory and use information to test it.

There are great problems in applying this method to a study of society, because society is not like a laboratory where variables can be controlled (as is often the case in experiments in natural science): it is an open system where control is impossible.

Natural science relies on applying falsification tests to theories. Social science, however, is concerned with the realm of social systems where variables cannot be controlled and falsification tests cannot work effectively.

## Facts versus opinions

Sociologists research issues in the real, or external, world, and collect data which is used to form evidence. The data is collected by one of two research methods: quantitative or qualitative research.

## Quantitative research

This is research presented in the form of numbers. Without such data conclusions are not valid. Sociologists who support and utilise quantitative methods argue that sociology should aim to be a science of society, adopting scientific research methods.

> It can be viewed as essential because unless human behaviour can be translated into numerical terms it cannot be measured and compared.

Take two schools: School A has 20 per cent of its pupils gaining 5 A–C grades at GCSE; School B has 40 per cent of pupils with 5 A–C grades at GCSE. What information do you gain from these quantitative statistics?

- A is a 'better' school than B?
- B has 'worse' children than A?
- B has 'worse' teachers than A?

What other information would you need before you reviewed your thinking? Would your attitude change if you knew that School A had better grades than B in the previous year? Possibly not, because you could say that it shows that School A is in decline. However, you do not know from the original set of figures everything about the schools and all the factors that go into producing examination results. Despite this, quantitative facts can be used to influence opinions about virtually anything!

## Qualitative research

The other main type of research is undertaken using qualitative methods – for example, an unstructured interview format could be used. This is more like a conversation, with the sociologist identifying the topic of conversation and leaving the person being interviewed a great deal of freedom to direct the interview where they want to take it. The main problem with this, of course, is then trying to compare different interviews.

Participant observation means that the sociologist joins a group in order to observe the action of its members. Taking the earlier example of School A/B it is possible to argue that an Ofsted inspector would be doing just this. Certainly, Ofsted could claim that the data they produce is richer, has greater depth, affords more insight and is more likely to provide a true and valid picture than other forms of assessment.

It is, of course, worth stressing here that researchers almost inevitably use a combination of *both* quantitative and qualitative analysis. Each can be seen as suitable for particular kinds of data and both can be used in the same research programme.

Quantitative research involves presenting findings in the form of numbers. Qualitative research often involves smaller numbers and an unstructured approach in obtaining data.

## Sample question and model answer

How far do you think you can tell a person's social class by means of
- Clothes?  • Speech?

How would you argue this?

*Edexcel specimen*

*The answer would need to contain the following elements:*

- *An introduction that should include some kind of definition of social class and a mention of the criteria that make up class.*

**Step 1**
Write an introduction.

- *Looking at clothes, you would need to give reasons why you could tell social class from them, for example:*
  - *cost*        *– type, e.g. 'green wellie brigade', Barbour jackets*
  - *style, cut*      *– label, e.g. Calvin Klein, Gucci*

**Step 2**
Provide reasons *for* the argument for clothes indicating class.

- *Then reasons why you cannot tell social class from them:*
  - *many clothes are uniforms; teachers in suits*
  - *cheap copies can be made of expensive clothes*
  - *factory production means quality can be purchased cheaply*
  - *many young people (and not so young) wear jeans and sweatshirts*
  - *global society means everyone wears the same*
  - *generally there are not class distinctions relating to clothes – certainly not compared with previous eras of history.*

**Step 3**
Give reasons *against* the argument for clothes indicating class.

- *Speech – arguments for being able to tell class could include:*
  - *type of language used – expressions, abusive language, swearing, etc.*
  - *complexities of language (possibly indicating educational qualifications)*
  - *accent; this poses a problem: regional accents have connotations; Northern or Midland accents are often used in the media to portray a lack of intelligence or sophistication. People who wanted to be successful in broadcasting (e.g. Sue Lawley) had elocution lessons to enable them to lose their accent*

**Step 4**
Give reasons *for* speech indicating class.

- *Arguments against speech enabling one to tell class could include:*
  - *many upper and upper middle class people swear for effect, which is different from lower classes swearing because they do not have alternative vocabulary.*

**Step 5**
Give reasons *against* the argument for speech indicating class. In your answer avoid using words like 'posh' or 'smart'. These do not convey anything to the examiner.

- *A final paragraph should come to some kind of reasoned conclusion. It needs to be noted that although your conclusion should be backed up by evidence, the conclusion need **not** be total – in other words, you do not have to decide one way or the other. When in doubt, be prepared to sit on the fence!*

**Step 6**
Provide a conclusion.

*Here is an example of an answer to the question from a 16-year-old student who has just started AS (i.e. she is in the October of her first year of post-16 study).*

*As you will see, she does not give an introduction and does not define social class. However, she does argue points both for and against the ideas for speech and clothes. She does inevitably use generalisations, but most of these are relevant. Her conclusion is rather thin and needs enhancing. However, in total, for so early on in the course it is a sensible effort, taking possibly 30 minutes and deserves a reasonably high grade. I would expect a rather more polished effort by the time of the examination.*

Effective essays will consist of an introduction containing a definition of key terms and/or a statement of what is to be covered, and the main body of the essay – often in two parts setting out both sides of the argument.

A person's social class can be judged by speech to a large extent because this can often reflect their upbringing – i.e. the area they were born in, and which part of the country. The different colloquialisms and dialects are often used to judge people's social class, as some accents 'sound' more common than others – even though it may not be strictly true. If a person was to swear/use bad language in an inappropriate situation it would mean people may judge them to be lower class because of the beliefs and values they have which go with their behaviour and the way they have presented themselves.

# Sample question and model answer (continued)

On the other hand, it could be argued that a person's class cannot be judged by their speech as it can be 'put on' or faked and would be therefore deceiving. Although the way a person constructs sentences and uses vocabulary may be a good indicator of social class as this is a natural factor and harder to 'put on'.

A person's social class can be judged by their clothes to quite a large extent as it is clear that people from different classes wear different clothes. This is for many reasons, e.g. different places to shop, money available to spend on clothes, types of clothes needed, peer groups, etc.

People in higher classes have more money to spend and can therefore afford more expensive clothes and also they can afford to actually purchase a larger amount of clothes, thus having a wider variation in wardrobe choice. The quality of people's clothes may indicate which class they are from but may be misleading.

A person's appearance may be used to judge their social class because if someone purchased or owned good quality clothes they are more likely to take care of them than someone who has purchased/received 'hand-me-downs' or second-hand clothes.

There is also the question of 'branded' or 'designer' clothes as these were once exclusive to higher classes, but middle class people are now also beginning to move into purchasing designer clothes and are moving away from high-street labels. Designer clothes are fast becoming popular to youth from all classes. However, fake or imitation clothes are on the market along with stolen goods which are available much cheaper and so lower classes can also afford to wear these clothes.

However, this is only true to a certain extent because there are always 'ifs' and 'buts'. For example, a working class family may win the lottery and begin to wear designer clothes, but this would not automatically make them upper-class. It can also depend on the individual as everyone has different beliefs: some do not feel it necessary to buy expensive clothes no matter what their class.

A personal opinion can often be given in the conclusion based on the arguments that have been advanced.

In conclusion I believe that a person's social class can be judged by the way they speak and the clothes they wear to a large extent, but not fully because other things need to be taken into consideration.

## Practice examination questions

### Short answer questions

***1*** Which of the following methods of investigation do social scientists often use:

(i)   controlled laboratory experiments
(ii)  questionnaires
(iii) interviews
(iv)  participant observation
(v)   statistical analysis

*Edexcel specimen paper*

***2*** What images of your present school or college, or of an institution of higher education to which you have applied, led to you choosing to apply for it.

*AEB Past paper (IV) 1997*

### Essay questions

***3*** What is meant by the term 'educational league tables' and how can attempts to measure the achievements of schools and colleges have both advantages and disadvantages?

*OCR specimen paper*

***4*** To what extent do you agree that 'wealth creation' rather than 'wealth distribution' is the best way to bring about a 'fair society'?

*AQA B specimen paper*

# Chapter 2

# Political concepts

**The following topics are covered in this chapter:**

- The political system
- Political parties
- Voting trends
- Pressure groups

## 2.1 The political system

**After studying this section you should be able to:**

- explain the concept of democracy and describe its evolution
- outline other forms of political systems that exist in the world today

LEARNING SUMMARY

### The nature of democracy

| | |
|---|---|
| AQA A | M3 |
| AQA B | M1, M3 |
| EDEXCEL | M3 |
| OCR | M3 |

Many students have difficulty in writing about the subject of politics. They feel that they know little about it, that it has nothing to do with them until they are eighteen and that adults are not interested in their views before that time anyway.

It is therefore useful to outline the development of the British political system, which is an example of a democracy.

> Democracy means involving all citizens in decision-making.

The idea of democracy emanated from the political system of Ancient Greece – the word 'democracy' coming from two Greek words: *demos* (people) and *kratos* (power), and meaning 'power to the people'. In Athens, in the fifth century BC, assemblies of all citizens were held to discuss important issues – this was a direct or **participatory democracy**.

> **KEY POINT**
>
> Democracy comes from the Greek words *demos* (people) and *kratos* (power) and means 'power to the people'.

It was this form of government that prompted Aristotle (the Greek philosopher) to comment that 'man by nature is a political animal'.

However, it is worth noting that even this seemingly ideal system actually excluded women and slaves (i.e. over 50 per cent of the population).

> Representative democracy: involves citizens choosing representatives who exercise power on their behalf but who can be removed if the citizens disagree with the decisions these representatives make.

To overcome the problem inherent in a direct or participatory democracy that citizens need to be there all the time to make the decisions, representative democracies were set up.

Democracy in its modern form has evolved over the last two hundred years. It is a huge cornerstone of the UK's political system because it is regarded as something that ensures we have an equal and fair political system: a **liberal democracy**. The right of citizens to elect their own representatives in regular, free elections is a basic ideal of liberal democracy. The citizens of such a democracy also have the right to individual freedoms (such as freedom of speech), guaranteed by an independent judiciary which helps separate powers between the policy makers, the law makers and the law interpreters (i.e. the judiciary). The UK's liberal democracy influenced the ideas of the American Revolution (1776–83) and the French Revolution (1789–1815). It also led to demands for the extension of working rights in the UK in the nineteenth century, leading to Reform Acts in 1832, 1867 and 1884 which extended the right to vote to virtually all men. In 1918 and 1928, Reform acts also gave the right to vote to all women. In 1969 the age at which someone could vote was lowered to eighteen.

Changes through Reform Acts of Parliament between 1832 and 1969 resulted in all people aged 18 and over being able to vote in the UK.

## Progress check

1  Why do you think that women took so long to receive the right to vote?
2  What factors led to women achieving the right to vote?
3  Why do you think the voting age was lowered to 18 in 1969?

You could have included the following reasons:

1  Through history men have held the power and, therefore, decision-making responsibilities; Women's roles were seen as submission to men and child-rearing and therefore their views were not considered; A feeling that women should not bother themselves with 'this' sort of thing.
2  The work of the suffragettes – you can find more about this in any encyclopaedia or CD-Rom; the events of World War I, which led to women taking over many occupations which hitherto had been male-dominated.
3  It was the end of the 'swinging sixties' when youth first had a real say; A generation had grown up after World War II who had the benefits of higher education and were more articulate and demanding in their desires; possibly the government of the day (Labour) thought that a majority of the new electorate would vote for them – ironically, the Conservatives then won the 1970 General Election.

## Other forms of government

| | |
|---|---|
| AQA A | M3 |
| AQA B | M1, M3 |
| EDEXCEL | M3 |
| OCR | M3 |

In addition to liberal democracy there are other forms of government flourishing today.

### Emergent democracies

Those aspiring to the accepted liberal democracy status. These include countries such as the former communist states of Eastern Europe and some African or Asian states where the army still remains an important political force – for example, Indonesia or Pakistan (where the events of October 1999 saw the army taking over 'to protect democracy').

### Communism

This still exists in Cuba, Vietnam, North Korea and China and regards itself as a superior system to liberal democracy. This is because it has not only given the people stable government and a fairer share of the country's wealth, but also freedom from unemployment, hunger, illiteracy and crime. (Communism, of course, does not provide freedom of choice.)

### Military dictatorship

This is where the armed forces undermine any attempt at civilian rule, for example, in Burma.

### Nationalistic socialism

This is always identified with Hitler's Germany, Franco's Spain and Mussolini's Italy and has its modern-day equivalents in states that claim to stand 'left of centre' and are led by a strong leader who heads the country's only party (e.g. Saddam Hussein in Iraq, Kadhafi in Libya and Mugabe in Zimbabwe).

The citizens of a democracy have the right to individual freedoms, such as freedom of speech. This is guaranteed by an independent judiciary. Such freedom is not guaranteed under other forms of government.

# 2.2 Political parties

LEARNING
SUMMARY

After studying this section you should be able to:

- list the different parties represented in the House of Commons
- describe the policies of the three main parties

## The composition of the House of Commons

AQA A     M3
AQA B     M1, M3
EDEXCEL   M3
OCR       M3

When representative democracy was established it was inevitable that representatives with similar views would start to link together and form what we understand as political parties. This has a distinct advantage for voters because it allows them a chance to choose between different sets of policies and, unless these policies find favour with the voters, they are not likely to be voted into power.

We tend to think that there are only two or three parties represented inside the House of Commons today. There are, however, many more. The current (1999) list looks like Table 2.1.

The figures indicate the different parties strength in numbers of MPs as a result of the 1997 General Election. The figures in Table 2.2 show the percentage of votes cast in the 1997 General Election together with the number of seats at the dissolution of Parliament in April 1997.

| Labour: | 418 |
|---|---|
| Conservative: | 165 |
| Liberal Democrat: | 46 |
| Ulster Unionist: | 10 |
| Scottish Nationalist: | 6 |
| Welsh Nationalist: | 3 |
| Democratic Unionist: | 3 |
| SDLP: | 3 |
| UK Unionist Party: | 1 |
| Sinn Fein: (Represented but seats not taken) | 2 |
| The speaker: | 1 |

Table 2.1 Parties represented in the House of Commons

| | % vote | | Number of seats at dissolution of previous parliament |
|---|---|---|---|
| Labour: | 44.4 | | 274 |
| Conservative: | 31.5 | | 323 |
| Liberal Democrat: | 17.5 | | 26 |
| Ulster Unionist: | 32.7 | (In N. Ireland) | 9 |
| Scottish Nationalist: | 21.9 | (In Scotland) | 4 |
| Welsh Nationalist: | 9.7 | (In Wales) | 4 |
| Democratic Unionist: | 12.3 | (In N. Ireland) | 3 |
| SDLP: | 24.1 | (In N. Ireland) | 4 |
| UK Unionist Party: | 1.6 | (In N. Ireland) | 1 |
| Sinn Fein: (Represented but seats not taken) | 16.1 | (In N. Ireland) | 0 |
| Speaker: | | | 1 |

Table 2.2 Percentage of votes cast in General Election 1997

## Party policies

AQA A     M3
AQA B     M1, M3
EDEXCEL   M3
OCR       M3

Many of these parties have specific agendas and policies which make them distinctive (for example, the Welsh Nationalists, the Scottish Nationalists and the various parties in Northern Ireland). Each off the three major (Labour, Conservative and Liberal Democrats) parties claims to be unique, but there is a great deal of 'blurring' at the edges and they sometimes struggle to find policies which convince the electorate that they are different from one another. One of the desires of all the parties in the 1997 election was that: 'clear blue water' could be put between the parties to identify differences between them so that the electorate could make a clear choice.

### The three main parties in the UK

#### The Labour party

Originally viewed as the party of the working class and has been closely linked with the unions. These roots lie in the struggles of the workers at the end of nineteenth and beginning of the twentieth century to obtain rights they considered to be theirs. Labour traditionally believes in:

- higher taxation, particularly of the 'rich' to ensure a fairer distribution of wealth

- a higher involvement of the State in the lives of people, particularly in areas such as health, education, etc.
- State control of the means of production, e.g. nationalisation of major industries including coal, steel, railways, etc.

### The Conservatives

They are seen traditionally as the party of the upper-middle and middle class who believe in:

- low taxation
- freedom of the electorate to use their surplus money as they wish
- little interference from the State.

### The Liberal Democrats

They have struggled for the past 70 years to forge an identity for themselves, having been (with the Conservatives) the dominant party throughout the nineteenth century and until World War I. Of late they have made some elements of a resurgence (gaining 46 seats in the 1997 General Election, although possibly this was because the Conservatives were so unpopular). They believe in:

- strong involvement with Europe
- extra taxation so that it can be used on items such as health, education, etc.
- a large element of tolerance relating to concepts such as freedom of speech, etc.

> **KEY POINT**
> There are three main political parties in the UK: the Labour Party (with its roots in the 'working class'; the Conservative Party (linked with the 'middle class') and the Liberal Democrats.

## Recent changes to the three main parties

When Margaret Thatcher won the 1979 General Election her selling of council houses to tenants led to a far higher percentage of home owners, who psychologically could feel 'middle class'. This, together with the effects of the Falklands War, led to a large Conservative victory in 1983. By this stage several prominent Labour party members had left the Labour party and formed the Social Democrat Party which after initial success merged with the Liberal party in the late 1980s.

Much 'in-fighting' among Labour ranks during the 1980s led to their new leader, Neil Kinnock, beginning to modernise the party. Further election defeats in 1987 and 1992, however, led to Kinnock's resignation. John Smith then took over as Labour leader and on his death he was succeeded by Tony Blair, who recognised the need for further reforms.

Amongst these was removing the fundamental idea of support by the Labour Party for state control of means of production (or 'Clause Four' as it was known). By the time of the 1997 election Labour promised low taxation, less state interference and a change in politics. The rest is history, with New Labour obtaining the largest majority since the end of World War II and putting the youngest Prime Minister of the twentieth century in power.

## Progress check

1 How is it difficult to tell the difference between the two main parties?
2 Why is it difficult to tell the difference between the two main parties?

1 You could have included the following reasons: similarity of policies, e.g. low taxation, support for the Welfare State; No real difference in presentation and ideas – possibly links with Europe would be the exception here.
2 Since this is a slightly different question answers could include: as class no longer dominates the parties, election manifestos will cover a variety of areas and opinions; changes in society are recognised by the parties, who aim their efforts at the electorate with ideas that will appeal to them – all the parties are aiming at the same elements of the electorate.

# 2.3 Voting trends

*After studying this section you should be able to:*

- *list the factors that lead to people voting for a particular party*
- *describe the effects of the media and opinion polls on voting*

LEARNING SUMMARY

## Factors that influence voting

| | |
|---|---|
| AQA A | M3 |
| AQA B | M1, M3 |
| EDEXCEL | M3 |
| OCR | M3 |

This section explains some of the reasons for changes in voting behaviour over the last few decades. It is very closely linked to the previous section and the two should be viewed as one.

National elections are probably the only time that the majority of people in the UK are directly involved in politics. (Even then, about 25 per cent of the available electorate do not take part.) So, what factors lead people to vote for a particular political party?

### Family

> Butler and Stokes made this assertion in their book *Political change in Britain, 1974.*

In the 1960s and 1970s, most political sociologists (e.g. Butler and Stokes) argued that it was the influence of the family that was a major determinant in which political party to support. In other words, children tended to follow the voting patterns of their parents. Arguably, this has changed as a result of:

- increased social mobility meaning that children's social class often differs from their parents
- greater levels of education, leading to children obtaining higher educational levels than their parents, and being exposed to different view points.

### Class

> In 'Why did Labour lose yet again?' – *Political Review*, 1992.

Traditionally class was a major influence on how the electorate voted, with the Conservatives representing the 'middle class' and Labour the 'working class'. Recent analysis by writers such as Ivor Crewe have proved that class now plays less of a role in political decision-making by the electorate. The best example of this is the Labour Party who have been consistently losing manual workers' votes for the last three decades (e.g. 1966: 64% manual workers; 1978: 50%; 1983: 42%). One of the major reasons for this has been the actual decline in employment in the manual sectors where Labour was historically stronger (e.g. in the coal industry, ship building, or steel industry). There is now far more employment in the service-sector than in the traditional areas. Many of these service-sector workers, especially if they are 'owner occupiers' could be more likely to vote Conservative. It could be argued that the Labour Party's realisation of this was an important factor in the changing policies and attitudes prior to the 1997 election.

### Gender

Gender was traditionally offered as a reason for certain choices – for example, until 1979 women were slightly more likely to vote Conservative than men. Since then this difference has virtually disappeared.

### Ethnicity

Afro-Caribbean and Asian groups are usually solid Labour supporters. In the 1983 General Election, for example, 90 per cent of Afro-Caribbean and 71 per cent of Asians voted Labour. However, it is unclear whether they supported Labour because of its traditional link with the working class or because the party is considered the most sympathetic towards ethnic minorities – with more role models inside parliament (e.g. Diane Abbot, the late Bernie Grant).

## Youth

Young people are often perceived as being more radical, more likely to be left wing and more likely to vote Labour (or 'New' Labour). Certainly in 1997 the young were targeted by 'New Labour', with every first-time voter receiving a video recording explaining why they should vote Labour.

> **KEY POINT**
> The exact reason why a vote is cast may be difficult to gauge. However, it is likely to be a combination of factors, such as age, class, gender, ethnicity, etc.

## Region

Until 1997 there was the famous North–South divide – with the Labour party being stronger in the north of England, Scotland and Wales. This was enhanced in 1997 when no Conservative MPs were returned in Scotland or Wales (although Plaid Cymru and the Scottish National Party as well as the Liberal Democrats returned MPs from these areas). In other respects 1997 also removed (probably temporarily) the North–South divide. This was because whilst the Conservatives clung on in their heartlands (for example, outer London suburbs) the defeat was so radical that many of the areas of southern England (where the Conservatives had been so successful in attracting the working class votes were lost).

Essex and Basildon in particular, where it was felt the 1992 campaign was won and lost.

> **KEY POINT**
> In the traditional North–South divide Labour held more seats in the north than in the south. The 1997 election saw this divide removed.

## The policies

It could be argued that this must surely be *the* reason why people vote for a party. We have an image that a particular issue sways the electorate at voting time. Certainly, all parties look for that 'issue' which will lead them to victory. However, this idea is rather too simplistic. For example in 1987, the issues concerning the electorate were: unemployment, defence, the National Health Service and education. The majority of the electorate were in favour of Labour's policies on those issues, yet the Conservatives won the election. This can be explained possibly by the relative importance voters gave to the various issues and the fact that most of the electorate attach more importance to their own prosperity than to issues which affect society. In 1997 one could argue that the issue was really to get the Conservative Government out of power and this issue was the factor that led to the Labour victory.

US Presidents are elected every four years for a term of office – the maximum they can serve is two terms of office i.e. 8 years.

## The leaders

It can be argued that we are becoming far more 'Presidential' in our elections. In other words, we are copying the American system.

There is much more media hype relating to the personalities of the leaders. For example, in 1992 Neil Kinnock consistently had lower ratings than John Major, the sitting Conservative Prime Minister. By 1997, Tony Blair was perceived as young, assertive, 'cool' and 'with it', whereas John Major was seen as 'grey' and 'boring'. Many of the electorate do not actually seem to realise that they are voting for their local MP, not the national leader, when they cast their vote. It is only when the party has sufficient seats that the leader of that party is given the opportunity to become Prime Minister.

> **KEY POINT**
> National political party leaders can influence the way people vote, irrespective of the fact that it is local MPs who are voted for in elections.

## The effect of the media and opinion polls

| | |
|---|---|
| AQA A | M3 |
| AQA B | M1, M3 |
| EDEXCEL | M3 |
| OCR | M3 |

### Mass media

Arguably the media is an increasingly important influence. Although voters do not perceive that they are likely to be swayed by any bias in the media, the party that uses the media successfully can make great inroads into gaining support. (For example, the use by the Conservatives of the Saatchi and Saatchi advertising company in the 'Let's get Britain back to work' campaign in 1979 had a great effect.) The famous comment in the *Sun* newspaper after the Conservative victory of 1992 'It was the Sun wot won it', because of their article 'Nightmare on Kinnock Street' the previous day, also appeared to be valid. Certainly New Labour took note of this. Tony Blair held long meetings with newspaper proprietors trying to persuade them how much Labour had changed. By 1997 virtually all the national press were either pro-Labour, or not advocating the Conservatives (exceptions being the *Daily Express* and the *Daily Telegraph*).

### Opinion polls

Extensive use of opinion polls can actually appear to influence the electorate. This means that people like to support winners and may, therefore, change their vote because of opinion-poll predictions. In 1992 it is possible that 'tactical' voting by Liberal democrats who switched to Conservative at the last moment (because they feared predictions of a Labour victory), could have altered the final outcome.

However, opinion polls are not necessarily accurate. In 1997, while they predicted a Labour victory, they did not predict anything like the size of the victory. Some countries ban opinion polls in elections once an election has been called.

> The mass media and opinion polls can often influence the electorate over which party they vote into power.

KEY POINT

## Progress check

What are the advantages and disadvantages of opinion polls both to the electorate and the political parties in the run up to an election?

You could have included the following:

**Advantages**: it is clear how the 'race' is progressing; you are aware of how people generally, or even specifically in certain parts of the country, are thinking.

**Disadvantages**: polls are always dated – by the time people have been asked and the results calculated, opinions could have changed; polls can be biased – the question posed can steer answers a particular way; they can have an avalanche effect, with everyone trying to 'get on board'; they can be inaccurate: most polls predicted a Labour victory in 1992 and had not perceived a change of opinion in the last three days before polling.

# 2.4 Pressure groups

After studying this section you should be able to:

● describe various types of pressure group
● outline the methods pressure groups use to pursue their goals

## What are pressure groups?

| | |
|---|---|
| AQA A | M3 |
| AQA B | M1, M3 |
| EDEXCEL | M3 |
| OCR | M3 |

Protective groups aim to protect their own interests, e.g. trade unions, CBI etc.

Promotional groups can be looked on as 'cause' groups aiming to promote a cause they feel is neglected by the government.

Pressure groups are groups that aim to influence political policy without actually seeking political power themselves. There are a few exceptions to this – for example, the Green Party in Europe – but generally this rule holds true. They differ from political parties because they do not put up candidates at elections, but seek to achieve their aims by 'putting pressure' on those in government – hence their name. Their other distinctive feature is that they are normally limited in scope, concentrating on a narrower range of issues than a political party.

Pressure groups differ widely in their aims and it is possible to divide them into two groups: protective and promotional.

**Protective groups** are brought about by a kind of common interest (e.g. Surfers against sewage) or experience (such as the same illness, like the Motor Neurone Society) or they live in the same area (Shelfield Community Association).

**Promotional groups** 'fight' for a cause in which they believe. Examples could include groups such as Greenpeace and Friends of the Earth who are concerned with environmental issues. Many groups hold moral views, which are often 'for', or 'against' something (such as FOREST and ASH, or pro- and anti-life groups on the issue of abortion).

It is possible for a group to fall into both the above categories – for example, the Terence Higgins AIDS Pressure group. Consequently it might be helpful to consider an alternative type of categorisation. Wyn Grant in the *Social Studies Review*, suggests 'insider' and 'outsider' groups, based on how they are treated by the government.

**Insider groups** are consulted by the government, and they contribute their view during policy making – for example, the knowledge and experience of teachers' professional associations would be useful in making education policy.

**Outsider groups** have less access to government departments and ministers – for example, the Ramblers Association, or under the Conservative Administration the various trade unions.

> **KEY POINT**
>
> Pressure Groups can be divided into two categories: Protective groups where members have a common interest; Promotional groups where a cause is 'fought' for.

Another way of dividing pressure groups can be either into permanent or temporary.

The former are generally formed to protect particular interests (for example, Alcoholics Anonymous, or the Automobile Association) or have a particular set of beliefs (e.g. Campaign for Nuclear Disarmament).

> **KEY POINT**
>
> An alternative division of pressure groups could be that of 'permanent' or 'temporary' where the latter would dissolve once completing their mandate.

Temporary groups can be local – for example, a campaign for a zebra crossing outside a school, or be one-issue groups which once successful tend to dissolve – such as the group set up to obtain justice after the death of Stephen Lawrence.

## How do pressure groups pursue their goals?

| | |
|---|---|
| AQA A | M3 |
| AQA B | M1, M3 |
| EDEXCEL | M3 |
| OCR | M3 |

Pressure groups use a variety of means to achieve their goals, as follows.

### Contacts with MPs and political parties

Some groups use lobbyists to put their case to MPs – and some MPs are sponsored – e.g. some Labour MPs are sponsored by trade unions, while some Conservative MPs hold company directorships (however these days both trade unions and the CBI are not as closely linked to their respective parties). The question of where influence stops and 'bribery' begins is a matter of conjecture.

### Gaining public support

This describes methods such as the use of mass media and advertising, and organising local branches to recruit members. One example would be an organisation like Oxfam.

### Demonstrating levels of support

Public demonstrations, petitions and lobbying Parliament are examples of some of these tactics. They certainly provide an indication of public support and can definitely influence government. One example is the Rural March in London in 1998 which persuaded the new Labour Government to look again at such things as fox hunting and the rural economy.

### Providing evidence and information to decision makers

As experts in their field, pressure groups can be used by the government as sources of information – for example, detailed information given to the Government by teachers (January 2000) contributed to the Teachers' Pay Award.

### Non-violent direct action

This means anything that stops short of direct violence – such as disrupting fox hunts, or stopping the export of calves to Europe by lying in the path of trucks. It can, of course, be difficult to keep such action non-violent.

### Violent protests

Sometimes these are very disorganised – like the Brixton Riots of the early 1980s, or the City Riots of 1998. However, if the IRA is regarded as a pressure group, then it can be viewed as highly organised. This raises the whole question of whether pressure groups can only be regarded as such if they operate within democratic guidelines.

Pressure groups are an essential part of the democratic process, because without them a range of interests might go unrepresented in both local and national politics. The existence of pressure groups can ensure that power is not monopolised by a small minority. With the state of the present government's majority it could be said that pressure groups now provide the only form of 'real opposition' to the government.

## Progress check

Name three attributes of a pressure group.

You should have suggested the following:
seek to influence policy;
do not want power themselves;
have a narrow focus.

# Sample question and model answer

'Party politics in this country actually hinders, not helps to get things done.'
How far do you agree with this statement?

**Step 1**
Provide introduction.

*The question asks you to balance out the advantages and disadvantages of having a liberal democracy inside a state, compared with other options. It obviously needs plenty of examples to fill out your answer.*

*Arguments **against** party politics for the political process could include:*

**Step 2**
Provide arguments against party politics.

Whips are Government-appointed MPs who ensure that MPs vote at the required time.

Pairing arrangements mean that by agreement, MPs from both sides can be absent from the House of Commons.

- *the length of time it takes to get any legislation through Parliament is a great hindrance – e.g. 1st Reading, 2nd Reading, Committee Stage, 3rd Reading, House of Lords, Royal Assent*
- *delaying tactics, sometimes used by opposition to halt legislation, e.g. 'talking bills out'; use of whips and pairing arrangements*
- *the way in which minority elements inside political parties can hold a large element of sway inside that organisation and hence closely influence the outcome of political legislation.*

*Arguments **for** party politics for the political process could include:*

**Step 3**
Provide arguments for party politics.

- *the time that legislation takes to become law gives time for reflection and analysis, ensuring that few errors are made in allowing bills to become law*
- *MPs, although they are representatives, not delegates, have time to answer inside their constituency to the electorate about proposed legislation – e.g. current views on fox hunting*
- *it allows minority parties and minority groups to have their say and put forward their views, which can and do influence the final outcome. One example of this would be the recent potential revolt by Labour MPs over some of the proposals relating to recent changes in welfare legislation, which led to some of the proposals being altered by the minister concerned.*

*NB It is worth noting here that you will not be asked to give your own political views or express support for any particular political party in any examination question. So it is merely useful to be up to date with what is current in the area of party politics in the months before you sit the examination.*

**Step 4**
Write a well-argued conclusion.

## Sample answer

*The following is a response by a year 13 student who has tried to weigh up the issues involved in the above question.*

*This is a fairly weak answer. On the plus side, the candidate has recognised:*

- *time allows opportunity for reflection*
- *some opposition is pointless – although he seems to think there is always total opposition: what about 'pairing' and bi-party agreement over items such as Northern Ireland?*

*On the negative side:*

- *there is an assumption that everyone shares the same opinion on fox hunting*
- *there are very few or no examples and very little factual knowledge is known*
- *apart from trying to balance the answer, the candidate displays little knowledge.*

*The student needs to show far greater depth and knowledge to obtain a reasonable grade.*

'Getting things done' can be a very frustrating concept inside British politics and it can be argued that many people see the present system as outdated and antiquated. The way in which the bill becomes law through the House of

## Sample question and model answer (continued)

Commons and the House of Lords takes a great deal of time, time which could be spent doing other things. The attempts to get the law on fox hunting passed shows this and everyone knows that banning fox hunting is a good idea, so why should all this time and delay be allowed to happen? The other way in which party politics slows everything down is that any party not in power will automatically oppose everything that the Government wants to do, just to slow things down and to make a point. So all the process seems to go on and on and ordinary voters in the country get turned off the political process.

On the other hand, I do realise that when a bill is going through Parliament it gives people time to argue about it and bring up points which could be used to change it. So in that respect it does help the way that politics runs. Also, why should the Government always get its own way and automatically pass all the laws? Why can't the minority parties have their say, put their ideas forward and help in the ideas of party politics?

So I think that the answer to the question is that I partly agree with the statement. There are advantages and disadvantages to having the present political system and I recognise this.

## Practice examination questions

*Short answer questions*

**1** The term 'ideology' means which of the following:

    (a) The way of life adopted by a particular society

    (b) The representation of things in an ideal form

    (c) A system of ideas which underlies social or political action

    (d) A set of ideas which is generally believed to be true

    (e) The generally accepted standards of a society which influence behaviour.

*Edexcel specimen*

**2** The best terms for describing the British system of government are which of the following:

    (a) consensual

    (b) totalitarian

    (c) monarchical

    (d) parliamentarian

    (e) autocratic.

*Edexcel specimen*

**3** Which is the best description of the voting system used to elect members of the House of Commons in the UK:

    (a) proportional representation

    (b) transferable voting

    (c) first past the post

    (d) postal voting

    (e) alternative voting.

*Edexcel specimen*

**4** Laws in England and Wales are made by which of the following:

    (a) lawyers

    (b) the electorate

    (c) the police

    (d) parliament

    (e) the government.

*Edexcel specimen*

*Essay questions*

**5** Do you think voting should be compulsory? Give reasons for and against your opinion.

**6** Is it possible for the public to influence the political process between elections and if so, in what ways?

**7** With which of the following groups does effective power lie in modern Britain? Give reasons for your chosen answer.

- academics (as gatekeepers of knowledge)
- politicians (as legislators and managers of information)
- media editors (as interpreters of issues and events)
- business people (as creators of wealth).

*AQA B specimen*

# Chapter 3
# Business concepts

- *Employment and unemployment*
- *Leisure*
- *Transport/location of Industry*
- *Workings of business and their impact on society*

## 3.1 Employment and unemployment

**After studying this section you should be able to:**

- list the causes and forms of unemployment
- describe the effects of unemployment on individuals, localities and the country as a whole

LEARNING SUMMARY

### Defining terms

| | |
|---|---|
| AQA A | M3 |
| AQA B | M1, M2, M3 |
| EDEXCEL | M3 |
| OCR | M3 |

Students tend, on occasions, to shy away from questions relating to the economy. For the non-business studies or economics students, the subject can have a mystique which is rather off-putting. Hopefully, we will de-mystify it in this section. However, before we start: a health warning. It is vital that the terms used are understood and defined accurately.

Take, for example, the terms 'employment' and 'unemployment'. It might be thought that the meaning of these terms is self-evident. Unfortunately, this is not so – even with the term 'unemployment'. The published statistics record all those who register as unemployed by 'signing on' each week at their local employment office. Thus, if two million sign on and the total population of the UK is 54 million with the **working population** at 28 million, then registered unemployment constitutes about 8 per cent of the working population. However, these figures do not show that more than half the population is economically inactive.

> The economically inactive do not form part of the working population.

The economically inactive include:

- women who do not go out to work, but stay at home to look after the house and family
- young people under 16 – the legal age at which people can be employed full time
- retired people – increasingly these days under 60, or the more traditional 65
- those in full-time further education, those in prison, those who because of mental or physical disability are unable to work
- People who choose not to work – including those who prefer not to work because their income from social security benefits is as great as, or greater than, the income they could earn from full-time employment.

> This group of people could be defined as the voluntary unemployed (i.e. they choose not to work given the circumstances in which they find themselves).

An official definition of unemployment (used by the Labour Force Survey) treats as unemployed: 'those of working age, available for work and who have been seeking a job in the last four weeks.' We therefore need to know whether or not people are using this definition when they refer to the unemployed.

> **KEY POINT**
>
> Statistics about unemployment can often be misleading. The most useful way to define exactly who is unemployed, is to use the Labour Force Survey's definition which states that to be unemployed someone must be: of working age, available for work and have been seeking a job in the last four weeks.

# Causes of unemployment

In his classic work *The general theory of Employment, Interest and Money* (1936), J M Keynes put forward the idea that spending was the best way to alleviate an economic crisis. In other words, the spending on weapon production before and during World War II helped to create the low unemployment, affluent post-war UK economy.

The 1930s was 'the' decade of unemployment, much of it emanating from the knock-on effects of the Wall Street Crash in the USA in 1929. It was, in fact, only the build up to World War II that rid the UK of most of its unemployment. From 1945 onwards, whichever party was in power, there was always the pledge to aim for full employment; an aim which was, in fact, unattainable.

This attitude appeared to change with the Thatcher governments from 1979 onwards, who rejected Keynesian economics. At this time the monetarist theory held sway, i.e. public-sector spending should be severely curtailed in order to control inflation. This led to an apparent lack of concern over high unemployment levels, with the accompanying major social costs and waste of economic resources.

Whichever theory prevails, there will always be some unemployment within a democracy. In any autocratic state (e.g. Stalinist USSR or Hitler's Germany), unemployment did not exist because the state had total control and ordered people where and how to work, i.e. the population had no choice in the matter.

> **KEY POINT**
>
> The Keynesian Theory of Economics (the belief that spending money is the best way to alleviate an economic crisis) held sway in the UK until the Conservative governments of 1979 onwards. Subsequently, the monetarist view, that spending should be curtailed in order to control inflation, was enforced.

## Forms of unemployment

There are different forms of unemployment.

### Casual or seasonal

This is found in areas such as agriculture (e.g. harvest labour) or tourism (e.g. waiters in UK seaside hotels).

### Structural

Changes to the economy can mean that whole areas can be decimated – for example, the decline of the coal industry in the 1980s because of cheap coal imported from areas as diverse as Poland or Columbia (where wages were so low that they radically undercut the price of British coal). This hit whole regions such as South Wales and Nottinghamshire, whose economies had previously depended heavily on one or two staple industries.

### Frictional

This is caused by the almost inevitable time gap in moving from one job to another. Linked with this is geographical immobility where a person will not move to another area because of social links. It was this concept that Norman Tebbit, a Conservative cabinet minister in the 1980s, had in mind, when he told people to 'get on their bike' in order to find another job.

### Cyclical

During a recession or depression, demand drops heavily and this can clearly have a great effect on employment. For example, if there is a recession, people spend less on luxury goods, and therefore the first sector of the work-force that feels the effects are the production workers in that sector; so expensive leather goods, for example, may not be sold, therefore leather manufacturers will be forced to make leather workers unemployed. In an area such as Walsall, which has a history of leather goods production, this can have a great effect upon the area.

### Technological

The introduction of new processes, particularly relating to automation and computerisation, that can be used in labour-intensive industries can have major repercussions on the numbers of people employed. In the last twenty years this has

**Primary sector** means extractive industries (e.g. mining, farming); **secondary sector** equals manufacturing industry (e.g. car production).

occurred mainly in manufacturing and production, both in the primary and secondary sector. Table 3.1 demonstrates this.

| | 1979 (000s) | 1994 (000s) | Change (000s) | Percentage change |
|---|---|---|---|---|
| **Primary sector** | 705 | 326 | –379 | –54 |
| **Secondary sector:** | | | | |
| All production | 8,642 | 5,314 | –3,328 | –38.5 |
| (of which manufacturing) | (7,073) | (4,227) | (–2,846) | (–40) |
| Services | 13,240 | 15,210 | +1,970 | +15 |
| All employees | 22,587 | 20,850 | –1,737 | –8 |
| **Self-employed** | 1,842 | 3,230 | +1,388 | +75 |
| Total workforce in employment | 24,429 | 24,080 | –349 | –1.5 |

*Table 3.1*                    Source: HMSO Annual Abstract of Statistics. HMSO Employment Gazette 1993

## Progress check

Study Table 3.1 then answer the following questions.

1 Which of the three sectors of UK employment is suffering worst in respect of unemployment?

2 Why do you think that the numbers of self-employed people have risen?

3 What do the service production figures tell us about the future of the UK industry?

1 This is difficult to answer. On pure percentages the Primary Sector is worst off; numerically the Secondary Sector is worse off. (One could think here about the phrase, 'lies, damned lies and statistics!') NB It is very important to be able to point out something like this to an examiner and this will gain credit!

2 Mainly because of: gradual reduction of large-scale employers; many employees made redundant are given compensation – a large proportion tend to use this to try and set themselves up as self-employed.

3 The way forward – as we become more of a global village, production work may increasingly be done overseas. As a result, many people in the UK will be employed in giving services to the rest of the population.

### Levels of unemployment

The level of unemployment can normally be taken as a crude indicator of how well the economy of a country is doing. When there is a lessening of demand for products and the economy is experiencing a recession, it would normally be assumed that there was high unemployment. Low levels of unemployment tend to be associated with a buoyant economy. It needs to be remembered that these terms 'high' or 'low' levels of unemployment are comparative. In 1979 the Conservative Party used the Saatchi and Saatchi advertisement: 'Let's Get Britain Back to Work' and this was seen as a major reason for the Conservative election victory. However, within two years unemployment had doubled to over two million.

Economists and politicians regard the level of unemployment as the state of excess supply of labour. This is measured more effectively by taking account of registered vacancies as well as registered unemployment. However, this in itself is difficult because sometimes firms do not advertise or notify job centres when they have vacancies, preferring to recruit labour by other means (for example, part-time work, 'black economy', non-reported work paid for in cash only).

> A useful way of viewing unemployment is as the 'state of excess supply of labour'.

KEY POINT

## Effects of unemployment

| | |
|---|---|
| AQA A | M3 |
| AQA B | M1, M2, M3 |
| EDEXCEL | M3 |
| OCR | M3 |

In order to fully analyse the effects of unemployment it needs to be viewed from several different perspectives.

On the **personal level** certain effects will stand out:

- loss of income
- loss of purchasing power
- loss of prestige amongst family and peers
- strain on family life
- loss of standard of living.

In the **local area**:

- When there is structural unemployment (for example, because of the closure of coal mines, ship-building yards or steelworks) there is a great 'knock-on' effect. Not only do many of the population have greatly reduced purchasing power, but all the small firms that have serviced the major industry will feel the effect too, with many of them forced into liquidation and causing further redundancy.
- There can be social problems with whole areas giving the appearance of being run down or 'depressed', often with increasing levels of crime and so on.

For the **country as a whole** the costs of unemployment can be very high:

- less income tax is paid – and National Insurance contributions
- less VAT is paid because of the lack of earning power
- more unemployment benefit needs to be paid.

Hence we are forced to face the question of 'For a Government is it better to contribute to keep firms afloat or should they allow market forces to decide whether firms survive?' This is very difficult to answer. Historically the Labour Party was seen as the party who 'bailed' firms out. This was known as a 'lame duck' philosophy by the Conservative Party. Certainly, recent Conservative administrations have not believed in helping out – rather they have preferred to re-train workers for other skills so that they are better equipped for the rapidly changing technological world of the twenty-first century.

> There are three main ways in which unemployment can have an effect upon a nation:
> - on individuals, who have less purchasing power
> - on an area/region, where small companies can fold as a result of a larger industry closing
> - nationally (where there is less income from personal/company contributions to national insurance and VAT, and increased unemployment benefit to be paid).
>
> **KEY POINT**

# 3.2 Leisure

*After studying this section you should be able to:*

- *explain the reasons why leisure time has increased*
- *list factors that influence people's choice of leisure activity*

LEARNING SUMMARY

## The growth in leisure time

| AQA A | M3 |
| AQA B | M1, M2, M3 |
| EDEXCEL | M3 |
| OCR | M3 |

Leisure can be defined as time in which individuals are free from other social obligations. It needs to be remembered, however, that leisure and its corollary, work, are not mutually exclusive – one person's work is another person's leisure (for example, a supervisor at a swimming pool).

There are also a number of intermediate activities (such as eating or sleeping) that are not clearly work or leisure. Whatever the definition of leisure, there seems to be little argument that there is 'more of it about!' The reasons why leisure time has been increased are described below.

> Leisure is 'the time in which individuals are free from other social responsibilities'.
>
> KEY POINT

### Longer holidays with pay

Until 1936 and the Holiday with Pay Act, people who took holidays forfeited their salary for the time spent away from work. However, nowadays most employees can expect three to four weeks paid holiday per year. This, in itself, has led to a greater number of people who are able to take holidays and also in the number of holidays there are per year (see table 3.2).

|  | 1971 | 1981 | 1991 |
|---|---|---|---|
| None | 42 | 40 | 32 |
| One | 43 | 38 | 37 |
| Two | 12 | 16 | 22 |
| Three or more | 3 | 6 | 9 |

*Table 3.2 Average number of holidays per year by percentage of population*

One would presume that the figures for 2001 would show an extension or extrapolation of the trends for the previous thirty years, as a result of:

- a decrease in those taking one or no holiday
- an increase in those taking two, three or more holidays per year.

### An ageing population

The number of elderly people is rising rapidly – see Table 3.3.

|  | Total population (m) | Over 65 (m) |
|---|---|---|
| 1981 | 56.3 | 8.5 |
| 1991 | 57.2 | 9.1 |
| 2001 | 59.2 (estimate) | 9.3 (estimate) |

*Table 3.3 The rise in the number of elderly people*

Many of the elderly take holidays (hence the rise in importance of Saga, an organisation specialising in holidays for the over-50s). People are living longer, are remaining healthy and fitter for longer and are able to take advantage of this in their leisure pursuits. The imminent retirement of the 'baby boom' generation (born in the aftermath of World War II) will see this section of the population continue to rise in number.

## The shorter working week

The number of hours which the average UK 'work person' does has continued to decrease. For example, in 1983 a full-time working woman worked 37.2 hours and a similar man 41.5 hours. By 1991 these figures had reduced to 36.3 hours and 38.4 hours respectively.

## Increased affluence

A 'honeypot' is an area of attractive scenery or of historic interest, to which tourists swarm in large numbers.

There is far greater affluence in the UK today and this has led to more holiday breaks, some of which are at off-peak times. This affluence is well illustrated by car ownership: by 1991 64 per cent of families owned at least one car. This increase in car ownership has given people greater freedom to choose where and when they go out for the day. The advent of the motorway system from 1959 onwards, the improvement in quality of the roads (despite what some may think!), and the development of the by-pass to avoid bottlenecks, have all led to a reduction in driving time between places. As a result people have been encouraged to travel further, partly for leisure purposes. This means a greater volume of visitors to areas such as National Parks, which can become 'honeypots' – and this can raise problems in itself.

Linked to greater affluence is a vast improvement in technology, particularly transport technology. Until the 1950s holiday air-travel was only for the very rich. The last fifty years has seen the use of charter flights which reduce fares. The build-up of international airports near to large holiday resorts has enabled tourists to travel in larger numbers and greater distances than before. As in all forms of communication nowadays, the world is a 'global village'.

> **KEY POINT**
> The reasons for greater leisure time being available nowadays, include: longer holidays with pay; an ageing population; a shorter working week and greater affluence.

## Progress check

1 What do you think have been the effects on leisure of the factors listed above?
2 Are there any groups of UK work people who work longer hours than previously?
3 What do you see as the major problems relating to 'honeypots'? What solutions can you suggest?

You could have included the following:
1 People can go further afield on holiday; the two-day weekend has permitted more travel; longer evenings and weekends mean that employees have more time and energy to go to leisure centres; etc.
2 School teachers; public house managers; junior doctors – recent legislation has reduced their overtime to 72 hours per week; for any overtime worked only 50 per cent of the amount per hour is paid (a qualified doctor is a junior doctor for the first two years after qualifying).
3 **Problems include:** destruction of vegetation; litter, vandalism, trespassing; congestion of traffic; heavy lorries and tourist traffic; wearing away of footpaths; conflict between locals/tourists; unsightly cafés/car parks, etc.
**Solutions could include:** fencing off certain areas; provision of picnic areas; closure of roads in high season; park and ride; scenic routes which separate local and tourist traffic.

## Factors affecting leisure

| AQA A | M3 |
| AQA B | M1, M2, M3 |
| EDEXCEL | M3 |
| OCR | M3 |

It is worth remembering that the subject we are studying is General Studies and therefore generalisations are inevitably needed and may not always be totally accurate.

There are various factors that affect leisure and, in particular, the type of leisure activity undertaken.

### Age

The choice of activity is largely shaped by the stage people have reached in their life-cycle. For example, many teenagers take part in activities which include 'hanging about the streets' (i.e. they don't want to stay indoors), drinking, clubbing, sports – both participating and spectating. These activities are perhaps chosen because of the amount of spare cash young people have and the comparative lack of responsibility they enjoy. Their leisure activities could change dramatically when they have a partner and family responsibilities. Similarly, the over-60s' leisure activities can be constrained by lack of mobility or lack of funding because of retirement. However, as indicated earlier, with more people living longer and increasing affluence throughout society, the image of the 'impoverished' elderly person reading library books and gardening needs reassessing.

> Age affects the choice of leisure activities, especially because of physical mobility and funding, as well as personal responsibilities.
>
> **KEY POINT**

### Work

Many have seen work as a major influence on leisure. In his book *The future of Work and Leisure*, Parker (1971) identified different patterns of leisure.

**Extension pattern of leisure**
Where work spills over into leisure time; arguably this is typified by the professional occupations (e.g. school teachers).

**Neutrality pattern of leisure**
Where leisure is a major source of life interests in contrast to unfulfilling work (for example, people in routine manual jobs, such as assembly-line production workers, may have passions for fishing or football to compensate for the tedium of their work-day routine).

**Opposition pattern of leisure**
Where the activity compensates for the hazards and physical demands of dangerous jobs (for example, a coal miner may enjoy gardening simply because it is relaxing after the stresses of the day's shift).

Another way of analysing the influence of work on leisure is to argue that sedentary occupations tend to lead to more active leisure occupations and vice versa. However, while it is possible to find many computer operators, for instance, who are members of health clubs, it must be remembered that their membership could be due to a whole range of circumstances such as concern for physical well-being, or a current craze or fad for health clubs, and so on.

> Work influences in many ways the pattern of leisure activities a person undertakes. This influence includes work commitments pervading leisure time, compensating in one's free time for mundane job activities and choosing a leisure pursuit that provides relaxation after a stressful day at work.
>
> **KEY POINT**

### Social class

It has been suggested that social class is a factor that has a bearing on types of leisure activity. Whether this is valid is debatable, although if for class we read 'high income' then certainly there is some evidence for this: there are very few unemployed or low-paid people who are members of a polo club, for example. Certainly, while some leisure activities transparently cross class divides (such as watching premier league football), others such as going to the opera or ballet tend to remain inside a certain social niche.

## Progress check

Suggest reasons why football is no longer the 'working man's game'.

**Answers could include:** costs of admission – triggered by wages paid to top players, etc; commercial interests influencing when games will be played (e.g. SKY TV calling the tune); corporate hospitality ensuring that many people watching are not 'true' fans; all seater stadia, which have partly eroded the camaraderie of standing on the terraces.

### Big business

It is possible to argue that leisure is increasingly dominated by commercial interests. Package holidays, theme parks, pop concerts, cinemas, hotels and restaurants are all part of a multi-million-pound leisure industry heavily promoted by advertising. The leisure industry is one of the major service industries and provides a large range of employment opportunities. This links in with the whole development of tourism. Arguably many leisure activities involve travelling to new destinations to seek new activities, sensations and stimulation. Leisure activities such as Disney theme parks, or the Millennium Dome, involve an element of virtual reality. This trend is being followed by museums. The Black Country Museum in Dudley, for example, allows visitors to walk around a Black Country village of 150 years ago, complete with church and public house serving beer (at modern day prices!). The Jorvik Museum in York even gives the appropriate smells of Viking times!

The increasing use of computer technology for leisure activities will only add to this trend of virtual-reality leisure.

> **KEY POINT**
>
> The leisure industry has developed into a major service industry as a result of leisure time being more available to the population.

### Tourism

As mentioned earlier, one of the major leisure activities is that of foreign holidays or tourism. There are several reasons for this:

- the increasing pressures of modern life means that people want to 'get away from it all'
- increased education
- a desire to experience other cultures
- advantageous foreign exchange rates, making holidays cheaper
- the unreliability of the British weather.

Before they were 'discovered', resorts abroad had very few tourists, few local amenities, poor roads, electricity, etc. – and clean, unspoilt beaches. Once a rapid increase in tourism began which was probably government encouraged, there was a large increase in local employment opportunities (with jobs in hotels, cafes, shops, etc.) and work in the construction industry in building hotels, for example. Once road improvements began, extra visitors possibly led to congestion and pollution.

If the increased trend for tourists in an area continued, the stage arrived where tourists overstretched the resources. Although there was better infra-structure there was still major congestion in towns; beaches were litter-strewn, seas polluted, crime increased and there was a large element of noise pollution.

# 3.3 Transport/location of industry

*After studying this section you should be able to:*

- list causes of current problems with transportation in the UK
- describe the reasons for the location of industries

## The development of transport in the UK

| AQA A | M3 |
| --- | --- |
| AQA B | M1, M2, M3 |
| EDEXCEL | M3 |
| OCR | M3 |

Although there is a close link between these two topics we will consider each one separately. Transport problems are currently very topical and it is therefore necessary to be aware of the historical background to these problems.

Until the end of World War II, the major form of transport for freight, as well as passengers, was that of the railways. The nationalisation of the railway system in the late 1940s seemed to emphasise this. Greater affluence in the 1950s, and the increase in automation in the introduction of motor vehicles led to a vast increase in the number of vehicles on roads in the UK. The introduction of a motorway system in the UK starting with the M1 in 1959, to cater for the increasing number of vehicles (typified by the first mini car in 1959), only exacerbated the problem: better roads encouraged more people to use them with a resultant diminution in the use of railways.

By the early 1960s the railway system in the UK was in serious trouble and the 'Beeching Axe' of the early 1960s closed down many unprofitable lines.

> Historically, the railway was the main form of transport in the UK until the greater affluence of the 1950s led to an increase in the number of vehicles on the country's roads.

**KEY POINT**

Inflation is the persistent tendency for prices to rise over time. It affects the behaviour of firms in the following ways:

- long-term planning becomes difficult
- profit margins become squeezed
- an increase in interest rates during inflationary periods hits firms with high debt-borrowing
- exporters find that the increase in their prices makes them uncompetitive.

The 1970s and 1980s saw a vast expansion of road transport, a proliferation of motorways across the country and railway use being largely concentrated on some freight and major routes between large cities. However, certain events of the 1970s and 1980s started to bring the dominance of road transport into question:

- The oil embargo by the Arab States in 1973 led, almost overnight, to a large increase in the price of crude oil and to a subsequent large leap in prices of almost all goods (because they were delivered to outlets by road); this caused many of the elements of inflation in the 1970s.

- The environmental lobby began to make its presence felt in relation to exhaust fumes polluting the atmosphere. They campaigned on such issues as:
  - damage to the environment in terms of both noise and atmospheric pollution
  - the impact on the countryside of an ever-expanding road-building programme.

  The results of the environmental or 'Green' lobby can be seen in such government strategies as:
  - lead-free petrol
  - the total elimination of four-star petrol
  - lower tax on lead-free petrol
  - lower road-fund licences for the smaller, less-expensive cars (i.e. the end of the 'gas guzzler' type of car so popular in the USA).

> The oil embargo by the Arab States in 1973 (which resulted in the rise in price of crude oil), together with pressure from environmental groups (especially regarding exhaust fumes) began to bring into doubt the dominance of road transportation.

**KEY POINT**

The 1990s have seen continuing problems:

- the possibility of total grid lock in major cities and on motorways (for example, the M25 at certain times of the day, or the M6 junctions 8–11 in the West Midlands conurbation)

- the privatisation of the rail network (supposedly to increase competition) has revealed an antiquated rail system in desperate need of huge injections of finance to make it efficient and effective.

The clarion call is thus for an integrated, well-functioning transport system that provides the service required in the UK both for personal transport and the transport of goods. The government faces very serious problems in making decisions about where to allocate resources.

Whichever way the government decides to move (and, clearly, this will not be totally in one direction), one of the results of the decisions made will be changes in how industries decide to locate themselves in particular areas.

## Progress check

1 What are the arguments both for and against keeping railway lines open?

2 List reasons for and against the rail system in the UK being improved at the expense of the road system.

1 **For:** As long as they break even (or better) in economic terms, they are worth keeping open in order to reduce road traffic; they provide a social function for a local area (i.e. the area is not cut off in times of inclement weather, etc.); it ensures that the area is not isolated economically.
**Against:** An inability to run profitably means that the subsidisation of the railway line leads to a draining of resources elsewhere in the economy; if people do not use the facility why should it be kept open for rare emergencies?

2 **For:** more environmentally friendly; if it is to survive at all it needs resourcing after decades of lack of investment; other rail services across Europe/Far East receive Government subsidies – e.g. France and Japan; updating is necessary from the safety point of view; it is necessary to ensure that the road system does not become totally jammed.
**Against:** however good/efficient the rail system, it is not as convenient as the road (due to being able to travel from door to door); increasing affluence means that cars are now available to a far higher percentage of the population and they have a right to benefit from this; extra roads will ease the pressure of congestion (past history does not prove this however!).

## Location of industry

| | |
|---|---|
| AQA A | M3 |
| AQA B | M1, M2, M3 |
| EDEXCEL | M3 |
| OCR | M3 |

Factors affecting the location of industry in the UK are as follows.

- Originally the major manufacturing industries were located to minimise costs of transport and to make use of natural resources. In the early nineteenth century the iron industry expanded in Sheffield because of the proximity of ore, coal, clay and mountain streams (which provided a power source). By 1900, steam and electricity powered the machinery and larger works were laid out on flatter land nearby. This meant that the product could be distributed by canal and rail. Steel is still produced in the area because, although the city location no longer gives a cost advantage, the technical skills of the work-force are important.

- The growth of motorways has made transport cheap and flexible, allowing manufacturing industry to move from its traditional areas nearer to major markets.

This is not a new phenomenon – in the 1930s firms were similarly tempted by government grants to move to areas of high unemployment: for example, the setting up of light manufacturing industry in the South Wales coal-field.

- The availability of government grants has become an increasingly important influence – for example, Enterprise Zones have tempted many firms to relocate. Central government has played its own part in locating some of its own activities outside the south-east (for example, locating the National Girobank in Bootle and the DVLC in Swansea).

- There is a growing trend for high-tech firms to locate in areas offering more advanced technological support (for example, Swindon and the M4 'Silicon Valley' syndrome, where local colleges complement the firms with training sessions for work-forces).

- Arguably, the availability of a large and well-trained work-force is not as important as it used to be because of the move by many firms towards more capital-intensive production. Another reason is the increasing acceptance by employees that they have to commute to work (which, of course, causes transport problems). If a firm decides to relocate it may need to offer a range of financial inducements to encourage its work-force to move with it. Conversely, a labour-intensive firm may be tempted to move to an area of the country with relatively low wage costs.

'Weight gaining' means where the end product is heavier or bulkier than the inputs. Conversely, 'weight reducing' means where the raw material is heavier than the finished product.

- Firms involved in 'weight gaining' production (such as breweries) are usually located close to their markets. Those involved in 'weight reducing' productions (for example, sawmills) have been located close to the supplies of these materials.

- Some firms are greatly influenced by the population distribution of their potential consumers (consequently locating close to densely populated areas). There are arguments against this, such as property and land costs.

- In certain industries pressure groups can operate both in a positive and negative way. The Nimby attitude ('not in my backyard') to the location of firms involved in less-attractive industries such as toxic waste is an example of a negative attitude. A more positive example can be seen in the fairly recent past when areas of the north-east offered substantial inducements to persuade foreign companies to invest in that area, e.g. Toyota.

- The existence of external economies of scale acts as a stimulus for firms to base their production in certain areas: the UK car industry, for example, has largely been based in the Midlands, thus leading to a supply of skilled labour and component manufacturers in that area.

## Progress check

What reasons can you think of that explain why industry is now more dispersed than was the case a century ago?

The following points could be made:

1  Industry is now less based on origin of raw materials because: (a) much raw material comes from abroad; (b) there are better, easier and more efficient transport systems; (c) better national training schemes for employees; (d) less geographical immobility exists than in previous generations; (e) there is more service industry – i.e. less primary and secondary industry exists, for example, the manufacturing sector; (f) the world is now a 'global village' (i.e. the influence of communications, or membership of the EU);

2  It could be possible to argue against point 1 on the grounds that there is more concentration in areas of high population, particularly as the old staple industries have died out. (One example would be the demise of the coal industry in South Wales which led to more concentration of industry in certain geographical areas such as coastal plains close to motorways.)

# 3.4 Workings of business and their impact on society

*After studying this section you should be able to:*

- list the various forms that businesses can take
- describe the impact of business on society as a whole

**LEARNING SUMMARY**

## Types of business organisation

| AQA A | M3 |
|---|---|
| AQA B | M1, M2, M3 |
| EDEXCEL | M3 |
| OCR | M3 |

> An organisation is a group of people who are brought together to achieve a specific purpose. Business organisations are firms or companies.

There are certain terms used in any discussion on types of business in the UK, and these need to be understood. Basically, a business is an organisation that usually requires buildings, equipment and assets in order to pursue their business. These assets are owned either by private individuals (the **private sector**) or by government agencies where the finance comes from public funds (the **public sector**).

> **KEY POINT**
>
> A business is an organisation where a person or people set out to achieve a specific purpose.

There are many forms of business organisation, as follows.

### Sole proprietor

Typical of a small business (for example, newsagents, plumbers, hair dressers), these are easy to establish and straightforward to operate. They are established on the owner's capital and often use only the owner's labour – and he or she takes all the financial risk. The market-place in which sole proprietors operate is usually very competitive and consequently banks may be cautious in giving them loans. If the proprietor employs other people he or she is responsible for all the financial commitments of the organisation, including the administration of VAT and personal taxes. If a business cannot meet its liabilities then the owner can be made bankrupt.

> **KEY POINT**
>
> The sole proprietor of a business runs all the financial risk and is liable for all financial commitments.

### Partnership

This is when a business is owned and run by two or more individuals. These are often formed by individuals who have similar skills (such as doctors, lawyers, etc.). A **sleeping partner** is one who contributes to the financing of the firm but plays no active part. All partners have to accept **unlimited personal liability** for the debts of the business unless they are protected by the Limited Partnership Act of 1907. Thus, although a partnership can be a way of spreading risk, it can also incur new risks.

Partnerships have the advantage of:
- providing a simple way of bringing skills and finance into a business
- thus enabling the business to diversify and grow.

Disadvantages are:
- unlimited liability
- lack of continuity as partners change
- management problems because partners have equal responsibility but may not have equal management expertise.

> Parties are liable **jointly and severally** – this means that the debts are first met out of the business assets and then, if necessary, out of the personal assets of the individual partners.

> **KEY POINT**
>
> Partnerships in business have the advantage of providing more skills and finance, although other issues (such as lack of continuity) can impede the progress of the business.

## Companies

Registering a company means that documents must be sent to the Registrar of Companies to show its purpose, its address, the way it is to be run and the names of its directors and company secretary.

Legally a body corporate: an organisation with legal status and separate identity from that of its members. A company has debts and liabilities, and it can own property, employ people, sue and be sued for injury or breach of contract. A company has to be registered.

**Public companies** raise capital by selling shares to the public. Most companies divide their financial capital funds into shares and are **limited liability companies**. The shareholders own the company, but large companies (such as British Telecom) have thousands of shareholders – most of whom will never attend a meeting.

## Franchises

This is where a licence is issued from one company (the franchiser) to another company (the franchisee) to allow it to sell or distribute certain brand-name products (McDonald's for example).

> A franchise is a licence issued from one company (the franchiser) to another (the franchisee).
>
> **KEY POINT**

## Privatisation

A 'nationalised industry' is owned by the state and run as a public corporation. The chairman and board of directors are chosen by the government and are responsible to a government minister who is accountable to parliament. A 'privatised company' has a chairman and board of directors responsible to the shareholders.

One contentious area relating to business in the UK in the last 20 years has been the issue of nationalisation and privatisation.

The privatisation of many state-controlled industries in the 1980s and 1990s has taken various forms:

- sales of shares to transform public corporations into public companies (e.g. British Telecom)
- council housing has been sold on favourable terms to tenants
- local services have been contracted to private firms (e.g. hospital cleaning).

Advantages claimed for privatisation are:
- access to normal commercial sources of capital
- improved business efficiency and profitability
- reduced pressure on public funding
- greater choice for consumers.

Arguments against privatisation can include:
- only profitable industries are privatised and this may not be in the public interest
- it does not necessarily mean freedom from government control because the government can remain the most influential shareholder (for example, in companies like British Aerospace)
- arguably, consumer choice is not relevant in industries such as water and electricity supply.

Entrepreneurs are individuals who are willing to take risks on the basis of a belief in their idea or product.

In the UK by far the majority of firms are small, sole proprietors or partnerships. Basically, a small firm can be viewed as an organisation of less than two hundred employees. While individually insignificant, these collectively account for 60 per cent of all employment. Large firms are mostly public and private companies and include the main household names in the UK. Much emphasis is put on small firms by government, partly because they are a form of entrepreneurship in the economy. Entrepreneurs may be managers, particularly in small firms, but in larger firms the manager's role may be quite distinct from that of the owner who is risking his or her capital.

## The impact of business on society

AQA A — M3
AQA B — M1, M2, M3
EDEXCEL — M3
OCR — M3

Business impinges on the way in which society operates in a variety of ways. Many of these areas have come to the fore relatively recently, as organisations and individuals have become more aware of both their rights and responsibilities. This, in turn, has tempered the attitudes of firms towards the profit motive. The issues involved fall into a number of categories.

### Economic

This relates to the question of how much government intervention there should be in a business system. While privatisation has heralded a lessening of direct government involvement, other facets of government have developed such as employee protection.

The Health and Safety at Work Act (HASAWA) 1974.
Under this Act employers are obliged to provide safe:

- working environment
- plant and systems of work
- entry and exit arrangements
- working processes

The Employment Protection (Consolidation) Act 1978. This protects workers under a contract from unfair dismissal. To qualify, an employee must work at least 16 hours per week for 2 years, or 8 hours a week for 5 years. Dismissal can be through termination of contract, through a fixed-term contract being completed or 'constructive'.

> Constructive dismissal means where the employee resigns due to the conduct of the employer.

The employer can dismiss an employee on the grounds of incompetence, gross or serious misconduct or because the post becomes redundant. Remedies for unfair dismissal include re-instatement, compensation or re-engagement in a comparable job. More recent legislation includes that of:

- the 48-hour working week rule, which states as a maximum the number of hours to be worked weekly.
- In 1999 the Minimum Wage Act (1999), by which there is a set amount for the hourly rate for each worker. (At present this stands at £3.00 per hour (under 21) and £3.60 (21 and over).)

> **KEY POINT**
>
> While privatisation would appear to herald a lessening of direct government involvement, other areas of government intervention have developed. These include: employee protection (through health and safety and unfair dismissal legislation), as well as the minimum working wage.

### Ecological

Problems relating to air and water pollution were touched on earlier in the transport section. Air pollution arises from both industry and motor vehicles. Carbon-dioxide emissions create 'acid rain' which damages both buildings and forests. The gap in the ozone layer is perhaps the most spectacular example of air pollution. Other ecological issues include pollution of rivers, beaches, etc. and the development of the leisure industry, which can contribute to pollution in the form of oil and other waste such as litter and noise. Business needs to consider all these problems, particularly when deciding where to locate new developments.

### Socio-cultural issues

> Organisations can be regarded as an integral part of society because of the influence they have on the structure of that society.

Since it is part of society, any organisation can be considered to have some obligation to help mould and achieve society's goals. Thus, businesses often enter into sponsorship of concerts, support exhibitions of art, contribute to charities and finance events, in schools, etc. This inevitably becomes linked with promoting the sponsor and projecting their image. In this way, self-interest and wider social interest coincide to mutual benefit. However, what would you do if you were a school in Nottingham to whom 'Players' the cigarette manufacturer offered sponsorship of a new sports complex? At this point, conflict between the product of the sponsor and the institution is going to arise. It is debatable whether businesses can ever act in a neutral way.

Ethics describes what is judged right and wrong in a society – hence business ethics are concerned mainly with the impact of managerial decisions on people both inside and outside the organisation.

Another point that needs to be raised is that of **business ethics**. If managers have the aim of maximising profits, where do ethics fit into this? For example, if a toy company can product cuddly toys and make 100 per cent profit, should the management aims be altered if they realise that the toys are produced in sweat-shop conditions in Shanghai where operatives earn £1 per day? There is a difference here between what is legal and what is right and fair. Is it okay to argue 'if our firm did not take advantage of the low wage situation in Shanghai, others would – which could drive our firm out of business'? The golden rule 'Do unto others as you would have them do unto you' may be impossible to apply at work.

Is this a good example? Many Asian people work hard academically .

Closer to home there can be disputes inside a business where there are alternative and conflicting value systems. If the head teacher of a school wishes to improve examination success and finds that many of his pupils from an ethnic minority background take time off from school for religious festivals, etc., what is she/he to do?

> Businesses have a role to play in contributing towards society's goals and values. The ethics involved in decision-making cannot be ignored by those with power in the business.
>
> **KEY POINT**

## Progress check

1 What are the advantages of franchising, both to the franchiser and the franchisee?

2 What do you see as the advantages and disadvantages of the minimum wage? (Any attempt to answer a question such as this must turn the question into: Advantage to whom? – the employer? the employee? society?)

1 **Answers could include:**

**To the franchiser:** business expands; most of the effort is put in by the franchisee; profits go to the franchiser.

**To the franchisee:** trading in a product or service that is already successful; little difficulty in attracting customers.

2 **Advantages could include:** it ensures a living wage for everyone; it ends exploitation of the weaker elements of society; there is direct comparability across the business spectrum.

**Disadvantages could include:** the minimum wage could become the maximum – what is the incentive for the employer to pay more? It can lead to unemployment – marginal elements of the work-force could be laid off; service-industry elements, relying on seasonal labour, could close completely (for example, small hotels in seaside areas); could lead to the temptation to move towards 'the black economy' with undeclared members of a work-force. In other words, the poorly paid workers are simply driven underground.

# Sample question and model answer

Using an area well known to you, show how the travel industry can transform the life of an area and of its people.

**Step 1** (Planning)
Identify what is required.

- *Identification of area*
- *Emphasis on travel industry*
- *Area and people*

**Step 2**
Clarify how/what you intend to deal with.

*Brief introduction, so that examiner is clear you understand what is required.*

*Items such as – how:*

**Step 3**
Expansion on how area has changed and why.

- *quiet, few tourists, few amenities*
- *congestion, pollution, rapidly changing infrastructure*
- *litter, vandalism, etc.*

*Items such as – why:*
- *popularity with certain age groups, e.g. Ibiza (18–25 year-olds)*
- *greater affluence allowing people to 'get away'*
- *increased transport technology allowing rapid communication, making such areas viable*
- *World is now a 'global village'.*

**Step 4**
Expansion on why area has changed for local inhabitants.

*Argue that there are plus and minus points for locals.*

*Plus:*
- *higher levels of employment*
- *higher levels, therefore, of affluence*
- *more contemporary life-style.*

*Minus:*
- *life-style/culture threatened or potentially eradicated*
- *employment can be seasonal*
- *employment in tourist activities can be seen as patronising and demeaning to local inhabitants.*

**Step 5**
Conclusion.
Attempting a balance of pluses and minuses.

*Is the change all for the best?*

*Is the popularity of the area transitory and what happens when 'charter flights move on elsewhere'?*

The following answer is a solid-to-good response by a student. She identifies a sensible area and goes through changes which the travel/tourist industry can make. Although her chronology is a little out (Ibiza was not quiet even in the late 1980s), she certainly emphasises the differences:

- lack of quiet resorts
- changes in employment structure
- traffic
- changes in demographic breakdown
- economic advantages to the local residents.

Her conclusion is rather weak – 'if it wasn't Ibiza it would be somewhere else'. Her comments on the travel industry have to be somewhat inferred – in other words she does not explain:

- why/how there is a proliferation of charter flights,
- why these flights are so cheap.

# Sample question and model answer (continued)

| | |
|---|---|
| Area identified. | An area well known to myself: Ibiza. |
| Changes to area. | As far back as the mid-late 1980s Ibiza was an area of peace and tranquillity, where the only people roaming around the beach were its natives and a few holiday-makers. |
| Reasons for change. | Then in the late 1980s – early 1990s a group of British DJs went there and discovered that the minimal club scene had masses of potential. Ever since then, each summer season in Ibiza, beginning in June/July and ending in late September, is packed full of hundreds of thousands of sex-mad night clubbers, who go to Ibiza for select reasons: sex, cheap alcohol, sun and the club scene. |
| | Although Ibiza still has some of its own traditional culture much of it has been replaced by the gay community and club scene. Gone are the days of tranquillity which used to inhabit the island and which the inhabitants used to cherish, here are the days of sex, alcohol and clubbing. |
| Employment changes. | In relation to jobs, many of the traditional jobs had to go: for example farming, to make room for more night clubs – thus resulting in some of Ibiza's inhabitants having to move elsewhere to continue their life, although it has paved the way for many jobs for holidaymakers (e.g. DJs, bar staff and exotic dancers): all of which enable people to live their life. |
| | Ibiza used to be a relatively quiet holiday destination, now the only time one gets some quiet is if they have earplugs! Ibiza is a place for the youthful. It has not much room for the middle-aged nor the elderly, but holiday destinations have to cater for their target audience, which in this case is the late teens to mid/late twenties. |
| Problems identified. | Traffic has also been a problem. The holidaymakers have to get from one area to another in Ibiza and so rent cars and mopeds, all of which significantly affect the environment and amount of noise which is ejected into the atmosphere (also including that produced by masses of clubs) and destroy land. |
| Plus points made. | Although this revolution has disrupted the lives of the inhabitants of Ibiza, one must not forget that the holidaymakers are putting money into the economy by means of purchasing food and holiday souvenirs – although not much money, it is more than if there were no tourists visiting the island. |
| Minus points. | However, it must clearly be remembered that lives have been disrupted, the tranquillity destroyed and it is now known as a place for cheap thrills and dancing. However, what must also be remembered is that if it wasn't Ibiza which was transformed then it would only be somewhere else, perhaps somewhere in England, which would drive away our tradition, inhabitants and jobs! |
| | The travel industry can therefore transform an area either positively or negatively due to the amount of disruption it causes and money it brings into the economy. |

# Practice examination questions

### Short answer questions

*1* What is meant by the term National Minimum Wage and why might it be necessary?

*OCR specimen*

*2* Which of the following UK groups experiences the highest rate of long-term unemployment?

(a) Pakistani/Bangladeshi

(b) Black (Caribbean; African and other black people of non-mixed race)

(c) Indian

(d) White

(e) Other (includes Chinese; other ethnic minorities and people of mixed origin)

*Edexcel specimen*

### Essay questions

*3* Why are there such wide differences between what people doing different jobs are paid? Is money the most important factor in helping to decide the kind of work people choose to do?

*OCR specimen*

*4* What are the arguments for and against the banning of strikes by public sector workers?

*AQA B specimen*

*5* Until the 1990s railways in the UK were nationalised. The government favoured a policy of privatisation. Regulations governing the operation of buses were changed to allow more competition. Responsibility for railway lines, signals and stations passed to Railtrack and train services became the responsibility of 25 separate companies.

(a) What is the difference between nationalisation and privatisation?

(b) Using specific examples of bus and railway operations from areas known to you, consider whether more competition has been a good thing.

*OCR specimen*

# Chapter 4

# Culture and aesthetics

*The following topics are covered in this chapter:*

- *The nature of culture*
- *What are aesthetics?*

## 4.1 The nature of culture

*After studying this section you should be able to:*

- *discuss what is meant by the term 'national culture'*
- *explain in what way Britain is now a multi-cultural society*
- *describe other types of cultural influences such as the Arts and 'pop' culture*

**LEARNING SUMMARY**

### The idea of 'national culture'

| | |
|---|---|
| AQA A | M1 |
| AQA B | M1, M3 |
| EDEXCEL | M1 |
| OCR | M1 |

We often talk of being 'European', or being 'British', or being 'Welsh', or being a 'Geordie', or some similar phraseology. Culture can take many forms, but some people believe there is a high culture – a form or identity that marks a nation apart from all others. If we accept this, in what ways do we define such a national culture?

One traditional definition you might like to consider is that a nation's culture has three clear elements – a common language, a common religion and a common history.

> Celtic languages still survive in Britain, so is there a 'common language'?

#### A common language

Great Britain cannot be said to have a common language, although most people in this country can speak English:

- The Welsh language is very much alive, and forms part of the National Curriculum in the Principality's schools. A majority of people in Wales can speak at least some Welsh – although only a minority speak it as the first language. There is increasing use of bi-lingualism – in road signs, and public address announcements, for example.

> Think about how strong the links are between language and Nationalism. Do you think language is a sign of nationalism?

- In Scotland, the Scots traditional language is still spoken. However, although the political support for independence has been stronger than in the rest of the UK in recent years, the Scots language shows no real sign of revival and only survives as a major force in the far north-west, particularly among the people on the islands, who have always spoken it. It seems that in Scotland, at least, it is possible to have a nationalist movement without the use of a Scottish language.

- Across the Irish Sea in Northern Ireland there is a resurgence of Gaelic among the Catholic community, particularly among those who would like to join with Eire in a united Ireland. Using Gaelic is a potent way of saying 'I want to belong to a united Ireland'.

- In other parts of Britain, such as Cornwall and the Isle of Man, ancient languages that had become virtually extinct are now showing signs of being revived and are receiving, to a small degree, some official acknowledgement. When you drive into Cornwall, for example, the county boundary sign has not only the English name, but also the Cornish name of *Kernow.* This reminder of a language actually older than English is also marked in the name of the pro-Cornish group *Mabion Kernow* – the Sons of Cornwall – which has its parallel in the more radical Welsh nationalist group *Mabion Glyndwr* – the Sons of Glyndwr (after Owain Glyndwr, the fourteenth century Welsh patriot, who declared an independent Parliament and tried to expel the English from

A **dialect** is not the same thing as an accent – this latter being merely a localised way of pronouncing English, whereas a dialect will use different words, or forms of grammar, which are often centuries old.

Is a decline of dialect inevitable in a world of global communication?

Does advertising lead to uniformity?

The Reformation was the movement that sought to reform what was seen by its adherents as the errors and corruption of the sixteenth-century Roman Catholic Church.

The Church of England was seen as the national church since the English monarch took the title 'Supreme head' (but this only meant something in England and Wales).

Guy Fawkes night demonstrates traditional anti-Catholic sentiment.

The rivalry between Rangers and Celtic illustrates modern anti-Catholic sentiment.

Can you think of any other equivalent sectarian symbolism?

A national church?

Wales). The English have in fact been accused of 'cultural imperialism' – of trying to force everybody to speak their language. There is certainly at least some truth in this – in Wales in the last century children were punished by their teachers for speaking Welsh in school.

It is also worth considering the survival of local and regional dialects. Dialect words will often be used with pride by people who have a strong attachment to their locality. Black Country children in the West Midlands who hurt themselves might therefore be encouraged to stop 'blarting' (crying), or a Geordie cricket player to 'hoy' (throw) the ball. Perhaps the decline in the use of dialect over the last half century or more was inevitable when you consider the rise of things such as national, international and, now, global communications, but are we at risk of being linguistically dominated by the United States? Is the power of international advertising affecting us to an ever greater extent? When the same product has the same name in every country you only have to make one advert! Think about why, for example, Opal Fruits have been renamed Starbursts and why Snicker bars have been renamed from Marathon.

## A common religion

If the case for common language being a definite part of British culture is difficult to prove, does the UK have a common religion?

- Ireland would seem to provide a powerful argument that it doesn't. The Reformation, the growth of a national British church, and the rise of Protestant groups had little effect in Ireland until settlers who had accepted the Protestant views of John Knox in Scotland were offered land in the seventeenth century, primarily in the good agricultural land of north-east Ireland. The intention was to introduce a 'civilising' Protestant population, but the effect (lasting until the present day) has been to create a minority population in the north-east of the island and this situation has led to more than a century of sometimes bloody conflict. The Victorian prime minister, William Gladstone, famously declared, 'My mission is to pacify Ireland' – more than a century later the hope of a lasting peace remains an ambition.

- Religion has not only been a force creating great stresses in communities in Ireland – the same phenomenon can be witnessed in other parts of Great Britain. Perhaps one of the more bizarre anti-Catholic ceremonies is the burning of an effigy of the Pope in Lewes (East Sussex) every Bonfire Night (November 5th), while other parts of the country satisfy themselves by burning an effigy of the Catholic plotter Guy Fawkes. Of far greater social significance are instances of 'modern' religion-based conflict, such as that in Glasgow between rival Protestant and Catholic football supporters of Rangers and Celtic, the two major local teams. In the late 1990s the then Rangers' player Paul Gascoigne caused great controversy when, after scoring against Celtic, he imitated a flute player from one of the Protestant marching bands of Northern Ireland in order to incite the Celtic fans (claiming that others had told him to do it and he didn't understand its significance). For their part, Celtic football club flies the flag of the Irish Republic as its club flag.

- It is true that in England the Church of England (or Anglican Church), first established by Henry VIII in the sixteenth century, remains a formal part of the fabric of state, but the equivalent Anglican churches in Wales, Scotland and Northern Ireland do not have this privileged place. The Church of England's regular practising membership has declined more rapidly than that of other Christian denominations in the UK – perhaps reflecting its declining role as part of what is seen as the 'the Establishment'.

- Consider also the large number of new religious groups, and the faiths brought by those arriving from the former British colonies around the world in

Remember the impact of other world religions on Britain.

the years following World War II. It is now quite common to see places of worship belonging to Muslims, Hindus and Sikhs, amongst others, in towns around the country.

### A common history

A country free from invasion for almost a thousand years – what effect has this had?

The third strand in the definition of a national culture we should consider in relation to the UK is that of a common history. It is certainly true that no successful invasion from overseas has taken place in Britain since 1066, and this can be compared with the situation in Europe (where wars have re-drawn national boundaries, creating or destroying countries with regularity). When we watch TV events like 'The Last Night of the Proms' and see hundreds of people – many of them young – singing 'Land of Hope and Glory', it seems as though maybe *here* lies something we might call a 'national culture' or a 'national identity'. Yet how typical is this group of revellers of the British nation as a whole – how many of those present, for example, are Black, or unemployed? Perhaps what we are watching is little more than a visual cliché – a parody of 'Middle England'.

Culture and nationalism – is this a dangerous combination?

You need to form a considered view on this that you could defend in an exam, or a debate of some kind if you were called upon to do so.

Can the idea of national culture be sustained?

And what about the words that the Proms revellers sing with such gusto? 'Wider still and wider shall thy bounds be set, God who made thee mighty, make thee mightier yet' – this is hardly the stuff of European, or indeed of world citizenship! If we identify 'high culture' with such assertions of nationality do we not run the risk of isolationism in the world, or worse? If all countries took the words of 'Land of Hope and Glory' and tried to put them into practice it would be a recipe for global conflict. Is such a philosophy acceptable today? Why do people take such a clear pride in singing these words? Should cultures try to assert their superiority over others?

We need to consider the idea that the world is now a 'global village'. It is not uncommon nowadays to visit the other side of the world for a holiday, and global satellite broadcasting means we can watch live television programmes from around the world. The idea of nation-states, each defined by a unique culture, is going to be harder to sustain. (You might believe the world is already becoming dominated by the United States – a kind of global 'Coca-Cola capitalism'.)

> **KEY POINT**
> A definition of 'High culture' as being a common language, common religion and common history is difficult to sustain in contemporary Britain.

## Britain as a multi-cultural society

| | |
|---|---|
| AQA A | M1 |
| AQA B | M1, M3 |
| EDEXCEL | M1 |
| OCR | M1 |

Nowadays we live in a country (or countries, depending on your views on devolution or independence, for Scotland, Wales and Northern Ireland) that very clearly counts members of many nationalities and faiths amongst its people. This has changed the way of life in Britain over the last 50 years or so. There are now more opportunities to experience a variety of different 'cultural experiences'. Many people living in Britain today do not give a second glance to Sikhs in their turbans, or Rastafarians with their dreadlocks. These two examples of cultural symbolism that have been transplanted in Britain from other parts of the Commonwealth illustrate the cultural variation and richness of today's community.

Racism is still a divisive force in Britain.

Institutional racism is the process by which racist practices and beliefs become part of the fabric and rules of organisations – often unintentionally, but sometimes as deliberate discrimination against racial minorities.

However, it would be untrue to say that the development of such cultural diversity has found universal support, and the level of racism in Britain remains unacceptably high. Among young people this is perhaps best seen in the Skinhead movement, a phenomenon that is almost totally dependent for support on white, working-class males, often coming from areas of high socio-economic deprivation – where there is poor housing, little work, high levels of family breakdown and so on. However, racism goes much further than this – the official report carried out into the death of Black teenager Stephen Lawrence concluded that high levels of institutional racism run right through British society and need to be addressed by positive action, not pious words.

This is an important question on which you should take a view.

So why do people have racist attitudes? Do we still have a collective feeling of superiority going back to the time when Britain had an Empire 'on which the sun will never set' (Winston Churchill), or is there a religious element ingrained into our thinking from the stories of missionaries who went abroad to convert the rest of the world to Christianity? What do you think about the idea of having laws to try to get rid of racism – should people be punished because of ideas they have about people from different countries and cultures? Why have so many Europeans believed in the stereotypes about White and Black people (which originated in White societies)? Is it possible to condemn the Nazis for their treatment of the Jews, while tolerating the systematic persecution of people with different coloured skins by British skinheads and others?

> **KEY POINT**
> Nowadays it is difficult to talk about a *single* contemporary British culture – we live in a multi-cultural society.

## Progress check

Try to think of ways in which cultural experience nowadays is different from that our grandparents enjoyed.

**Examples might include:** popular music affected by styles from around the world, such as Latin or reggae; a wide variety of places of worship; an opportunity to experience different Art forms, e.g. Indian dance, Oriental art; restaurants and cafes serving styles of food and drink from every continent.

## Culture in the Arts

AQA A    M1
AQA B    M2
EDEXCEL    M1
OCR    M1

If there are difficulties in clearly defining an identifiable British culture in national or racial terms, is it more profitable to look to the Arts – to music, literature and art? Shakespeare is known the world over, and thought of as being at the heart of British culture (or English culture, at least), but how many people in this country read Shakespeare for fun?

'Shakespeare for the masses' sounds almost derogatory – yet if his writing is at the heart of our culture, why shouldn't his work be made more accessible. Why shouldn't it be adapted to other times, places and forms – for example *Romeo and Juliet* became the inspiration for Leonard Bernstein's 'West Side Story' (in which the rival factions are not the Montague and Capulet families of Verona, but rival gangs – the Sharks and the Jets in downtown New York).

Culture from experts?

However, pure art, theatre, music and so on have a host of 'experts' and 'critics' who define and explain it. If it *is* the Arts that provides our unique identification in the world, perhaps we do need to have such experts to interpret it for us. If the Arts lack mystique, or are not sufficiently serious as to need an academic explanation, perhaps they cannot be a serious foundation on which a national culture can be based. Many people take the view that we *do* need a body of Arts that defines our national consciousness, even if we ourselves don't know much about these in any depth.

So, is it in its music, writing and art that the defining soul of a nation can be found? They certainly help to reinforce local culture – for example in song, readily identified with certain areas – such as 'Blaydon Races' on Tyneside, a song that has been sung on the terraces at Newcastle soccer club for many years. Through ready identification with such music, or with famous writing or painting we can feel an identification and a pride – whether with a region or the country as a whole.

Gaining an identity through the Arts.

> **KEY POINT**
> Writers, painters and musicians from our national history play a major role in defining our culture.

## Some major British contributors to the history of the Arts

| AQA A | M1 |
|-------|-----|
| AQA B | M2 |
| EDEXCEL | M1 |
| OCR | M1 |

*Always reinforce points you make in the exam through examples and discussion.*

There are many examples of famous British writers, composers and artists. The following lists provide just a few names.

All these people have made a major impression on our national culture and their work continues to do so. If you are answering a question on the Arts in your General Studies exam you should always try to write about a range of examples to reinforce the points you are making. There are, of course, many other writers, composers and painters who have not been named here who you could choose to write about. You might be more at ease discussing the writing of Thomas Hardy, or the watercolour paintings of Turner, for example. It is not naming individuals that is so important as being aware of the role of the Arts in shaping our national consciousness and in helping to develop our feeling of culture. You might equally well illustrate an exam answer by reference to other practitioners than those listed, or to broader examples of types of writing, music or art.

*Writers: try to name at least one thing they have written.*

*Composers: much music has been written for religious purposes over the centuries, why might this be?*

*Artists: Painting creates an immediate impression, so can be a very powerful reflection of a national identity.*

| Literature | |
|------------|-----|
| Geoffrey Chaucer: Religious allegory and ballads | *13th century* |
| William Shakespeare: Plays, poetry | *16th century* |
| John Donne: Metaphysical poetry | *17th century* |
| Daniel Defoe: Novels | *18th century* |
| William Wordsworth: Poetry | *19th century* |
| Charlotte Brontë: Romantic novels | *19th century* |
| Charles Dickens: Social commentary novels | *19th century* |
| **Music** | |
| William Byrd: Sacred music | *16th/17th century* |
| Henry Purcell: Early secular music | *17th century* |
| Edward Elgar: Romantic, modern music | *19th/20th century* |
| Ralph Vaughan-Williams: Romantic, modern music | *20th century* |
| Benjamin Britten: Modern, sometimes impressionistic | *20th century* |
| **Art** | |
| Joshua Reynolds: Portraits | *18th century* |
| Thomas Gainsborough: Classical watercolours | *18th century* |
| John Constable: Landscapes | *18th/19th century* |
| John Millais: Influenced by Impressionists | *19th century* |
| Holman Hunt: Pre-Raphaelite Brotherhood | *19th century* |

## Pop Culture

| AQA A | M1 |
|-------|-----|
| AQA B | M2 |
| EDEXCEL | M1 |
| OCR | M1 |

Another phenomenon to emerge in society in the years since the end of World War II is what has been described as 'pop culture' (pop music, pop art and modern dance). Much pop culture is anathema to those who support the concept of 'high culture'. Perhaps the most immediate difference between the two is the more immediate accessibility of pop culture. However, the gurus of pop culture would not accept that this means it is any less relevant or meaningful. These two forms of culture involve people at different levels.

Official culture, preserved in art galleries, museums and university courses, demands cultivated tastes and formally imparted knowledge. It demands moments of attention that are separated from the run of daily life. Popular culture, meanwhile, mobilises the tactile, the incidental, the transitory, the expendable.

*Chambers, 1990*

> Pop culture might be far more accessible than, and lacks, the 'mystique' of high culture, but it cannot be dismissed as being of no importance, and it can certainly play a role in defining the beliefs and aspirations of many, especially the young.

KEY POINT

## Progress check

1 What three elements are sometimes said to be at the foundation of a nation's culture?
2 Name a part of Great Britain where historic culture has divided communities?
3 How does the 'Last Night of the Proms' concert reflect traditional British culture?
4 How does 'pop culture' differ from traditional 'high culture'?

You could have suggested the following:

1 Common language, common religion, common history.
2 The most obvious area is Northern Ireland, divided along sectarian lines since the military defeat of the Catholic army in the 17th century.
3 The music relies heavily on English 'nationalist' composers, such as Vaughan Williams and Elgar.
4 In simple terms it is direct, immediate and uses the here and now in a way that does not necessarily need any great insight to appreciate it.

# 4.2 What are aesthetics?

## After studying this section you should be able to:

- *explain what is meant by the term aesthetics*
- *discuss why people seek aesthetic experiences*
- *describe ways in which Art can be misused*

LEARNING SUMMARY

## The purpose of aesthetic experiences

| | |
|---|---|
| AQA A | M1 |
| AQA B | M2 |
| EDEXCEL | M1 |
| OCR | M1 |

We seek out aesthetic pleasure because it is rewarding – how could this be explained in a General Studies exam?

Put simply, the study of 'aesthetics' can be defined as the study of the philosophy of the Arts. It is the process of trying to establish what makes something good, uplifting or inspirational – whether it is a piece of art, music, literature, fashion or any other element of artistic experience. We need to start by thinking about why we read books, go to the theatre, visit galleries and so on. Do such activities make us into 'better people' – or is there simply a rewarding experience to be gained from such activities? In comparing and contrasting different artists and musicians, can we say that one is better than another? (Swings of cultural fashion will periodically make individual artists more, or less, popular over time.) Whatever our particular preferences, everyone seeks out aesthetic experiences – the opportunity to enjoy ourselves through the Arts. In this way a quality is added to our lives that would otherwise not be there. This may not make us become 'better' people in a social, or moral way, but we do gain some kind of enrichment in our lives.

### The classical versus the contemporary

You needn't worry too much if you know little about 'classical' forms of music, writing or art. The best modern examples (those that represent the high spots of contemporary Arts in any decade – rather than those that are 'one-hit wonders'), will stand up to analysis. For example, Paul Griffiths, who was once the music critic of *The Times* and author of books on classical composers such as Bartok and Messiaen, said in his book *Cambridge Cultural History* (Griffiths 1992) about The Beatles album 'Sergeant Pepper's Lonely Hearts Club Band' that this:

was the climax of their achievement. No longer simply a chaos of songs, Sergeant Pepper is a dramatic cycle, linked by the concept that the songs are sung by the band named in the title, and arranged with a carefulness for connection and contrast unusual in anthology records. The use of studio techniques normally associated with electronic music had begun in [their album] 'Revolver' (1966), as had the extension of subject matter far beyond the usual range of love songs, and the parallel extension of musical means: Paul McCartney's 'Eleanor Rigby' is concerned with loneliness, and occupies the Dorian modality of a folksong, with accompaniment for string quartet. But Sergeant Pepper goes much further, drawing in a full symphony orchestra as well as influences from Indian music, and concerning itself with the expansion of self-awareness that the Beatles had discovered through drugs, through Indian mysticism, and perhaps not least through their freedom to undertake musical experiment.

## Defining beauty

| | |
|---|---|
| AQA A | M1 |
| AQA B | M2, M3 |
| EDEXCEL | M1 |
| OCR | M1 |

> Language itself can be limiting in trying to describe our feelings and emotions.

**Beauty** is a word that encompasses a wide range of meaning. In other languages a variety of words exist to express the feeling of awe and grandeur that witnessing beautiful things can evoke. For some people beauty exists in magnificent landscapes: New England during the Fall, Provence in the bright sunshine of high Summer, or the bleak majesty of the Scottish highlands. Beauty can also be seen in things that are much smaller – the plumage of a brightly coloured bird, the mournful song of a whale, or the sound of a waterfall. Because the experience of seeing is subjective, there can be problems in knowing what two different people using the word are trying to convey. Some people might find mournful music 'beautiful' when others would describe it as 'depressing'. Nonetheless, although language can be limiting, it can give some indication of the emotions people experience.

> **KEY POINT**
>
> People may use the word 'beautiful' to describe a range of feelings – from happiness to sorrow. Because this word is used to describe a multitude of experiences, we cannot be sure that other people are feeling exactly the same as us when they use it.

## Progress check

1  How might we define the study of aesthetics?
2  What are some of the factors we might look for in, for example, describing a painting of a landscape as 'good'?

You may have suggested the following:
1  'The study of the philosophy of the Arts'.
2  The use of light, colour, perspective – capable of individual analysis in addition to considering the whole picture that is created. Its impact on human emotions might also be taken into account.

## Sample question and model answer

**Step 1**
Introduction.

Remember that only a sentence or two will be needed as an introduction.

Keep your analysis of national culture separate from a definition of nationalism – this is for the latter part of the answer.

**Step 2**
Development.

Move on to the idea of nationalism, seeking to be objective at all times.

**Step 3**
Conclusion.

Provided that you refer to points made, you can bare your soul in the conclusion to a question such as this one.

**Does the idea of a 'national culture' mean the same thing as 'nationalism'?**

- *Start with a brief word about how 'national culture' might be defined – perhaps in a nation's history, language, or religion; perhaps through its music, art and literature or maybe a combination of these aspects.*

- *You might choose to use your own country, or another you know well as a base for your answer – so long as you make it clear you are doing this, it is fine.*

- *Look at each aspect you have outlined in your introduction in rather more detail, suggesting ways in which it has helped to create a national identity.*

- *You might consider how language, religion, history create a sharper focus on a national culture – religious paintings, music composed in honour of specified events, for example.*

- *Having done this, seek to define 'nationalism' – the idea of the individual nation standing alone – and how this concept might be developed and boosted through its traditions, its arts and so on.*

- *There are undoubted links between national culture and nationalism, but do they have to be there – can you have a national culture without being a nation? Many in Wales would assert this is possible without full independence from the United Kingdom.*

- *On the other hand, you might point out that some extremist government – the Nazis or the Soviet Union in the Stalin era – have utilised their arts and culture in a very direct way to bolster the idea of a national consciousness.*

- *In your conclusion you need to draw together the points you have made.*

- *This becomes your opportunity to put your personal viewpoint – a clear indication of where you stand (provided it is supported by points made in the main part of your answer) will be well rewarded.*

- *Do not let your answer fizzle out – be firm and let the examiner know what you believe.*

*An example of a conclusion is as follows:*

In conclusion, I would say that when I hear music like 'Land of Hope of Glory', or watch a play by William Shakespeare, I need no reminder of my Englishness. It is in music, literature and the arts that my culture is defined – others might add factors like attending the Church of England. These things give me a feeling of belonging, of pride in my country. However, this does not for one second make me feel superior to people from other cultures, or that England is a better country than others. These latter feelings are often engendered by a slavish belief in nationalism. National culture and nationalism are very different things and to try to link the latter with the former is a great abuse of those things that help to shape our identity within the broader concept of 'the family of man'.

## Practice examination questions

### Short answer questions

1  Name three areas of the United Kingdom where old Celtic languages are showing signs of revival.

2  Which play features the rival families of the Montagues and the Capulets, and in which twentieth-century musical adaptation of the story are these represented by two rival sides of the Sharks and the Jets?

3  With what form of the Arts would you associate William Byrd and Henry Purcell?

### Essay question

4  What are some of the challenges and opportunities presented by living in a multi-cultural society in contemporary Britain?

# Chapter 5

# Beliefs, values and morals

**The following topics are covered in this chapter:**

- *Religion in the UK*
- *Values*
- *Morals*

## 5.1 Religion in the UK

**After studying this section you should be able to:**

- *describe the nature of religious tolerance in the UK*
- *outline the role of religion in the state education system*
- *identify important features of the main religious groups to be found in the UK*

**LEARNING SUMMARY**

### The influence of religion in the UK

| | |
|---|---|
| AQA A | M1 |
| AQA B | M2 |
| EDEXCEL | M1 |
| OCR | M1 |

Protestant groups were founded following *protests* against what was seen as the corruption of the church based in Rome.

Anti-Semitism – intolerance towards Jews – is not a new thing.

Many diverse religious groups can now be found in the UK – think of your own community or nearby large towns.

The United Kingdom has been primarily Christian since Saxon times. Following the Reformation in the sixteenth century a range of **Protestant groups** have existed, while in the last few decades a number of new and sometimes radical Christian sects and groups have come into existence. (We go on to consider the history of Christianity in Britain in more detail in a later section.) There have also been followers of other religions living in the UK for centuries. The Jewish community is the longest-standing example – the first recorded 'pogrom' (destruction of a Jewish community) was carried out, not by the Nazis, but by the English population of York in the twelfth century. (The Jewish population of the city took refuge in a church from the mob, who proceeded to burn the church, thus murdering all those inside.) The current Jewish population in Britain can be traced back to the seventeenth century when they came in large part to escape persecution in Europe, at a time when attitudes to Jews in Britain had become more relaxed.

Since the onset of large-scale immigration in the 1950s, hundreds of thousands of Hindus, Sikhs and Muslims have moved to Britain and often their families here maintained their religious traditions. Temples and mosques can now be found in virtually all large towns. Few people in Britain switch from one religious tradition to another. Generally speaking, there has been a steady decline in Christian observance, while the number of practising Muslims is growing – in large part because Muslim families tend to be larger on average.

> Key dates in the growth of religious tolerance in the UK:
>
> **1677** The Ecclesiastical Jurisdiction Act ended heresy being a legal offence.
>
> **1688** The Toleration Act gave freedom of worship to Protestant minority groups.
>
> **1828** Repeal of the Test and Corporation Acts gave non-conformists (Protestants who are not members of the Church of England) full political rights so they could hold public office.
>
> **1829** The Roman Catholic Relief Act gave political rights to Catholics.
>
> **1854/56/71** Religious tests on staff and students at the Universities of Oxford, Cambridge and Durham (requiring them to declare allegiance to the Church of England before they could enrol) were successfully abolished.
>
> **1858** The Jewish Relief Act enabled Jews to become MPs.

**KEY POINT**

Elementary education was a basic free education for pupils at schools in their local village or town community. (Successful pupils could leave from the age of 12, if they reached the required standard.)

## Church schools

Christian groups have been heavily involved in the development of education in the UK, particularly since the nineteenth century, when church provision pre-dated that of local authorities. The latter did not have a statutory role until the foundation of School Boards with the 1870 Education Act, which made Elementary education compulsory. Even when the Act was passed the churches were given a period to try to build schools where there was a need, until the School Boards had to step in. (The churches would have liked to have been given the chance to build more schools – hence the period of grace – but in the new urban areas in particular, the influence of the churches was minimal and they could never have realised sufficient capital to build enough schools.)

You may like to consider whether this fact sits easily with the idea of state education, in a country where many such schools serve populations made up of families belonging to a wide range of faiths.

Today, many church schools – particularly the primary schools that are the modern successors of elementary schools – still survive, especially in rural areas. Some such schools are financed virtually entirely by the church, but the majority receive their funding from local authorities, despite still having links with their local church. There are also around 2,500 Roman Catholic schools in Britain, and the Roman Catholic church attaches great importance to the education of its children in the Roman Catholic faith. About a third of all schools in the UK are church schools of some kind.

Other religious groups have also established a number of private, fee-paying schools. Among the most recent to gain a national reputation is the Islamia school for Muslims in London. Some prominent public (i.e. fee-paying) schools are owned and funded by different Christian denominations.

## Religion in state schools

The National Curriculum was introduced by the government in the Education Reform Act 1988. For the first time it set out the subjects and their contents that all schools (other than fee-paying schools) had to teach, and in which pupils are tested at the ages of 7, 11, 14 and 16.

From 1944 until the passing of the Education Reform Act (ERA) in 1988 the only compulsory subject in British schools was Religious Education – although since then the National Curriculum, setting out other subjects that must be taught, has been put in place. Since the ERA in 1988, every Local Education Authority has to have an approved syllabus of RE, and a Standing Advisory Council for Religious Education (SACRE) to be responsible for monitoring the subject, and the daily assemblies held in schools. The syllabus is determined locally, but has to reflect the fact that British religious traditions are primarily Christian. At the same time, the syllabus must be non-denominational (except in church schools), and must also acknowledge comparative religion – i.e. the study of the teaching and practices of the other main religions found in Britain within the context of a multi-cultural nation.

Schools must also hold a daily act of collective worship for staff and pupils. This contrasts sharply with many countries, such as the United States – where it is illegal to bring Christianity specifically into the school day. (However, in some parts of the USA the 'creationist theory' of the world has to be taught, and in Texas the Theory of Evolution has been removed from the syllabus altogether.) However, if a majority of pupils belong to faiths other than Christianity, and most parents want it, the governors of the school can apply to the local SACRE for exemption from the need to provide a primarily Christian form of worship. A daily religious assembly still has to be held, but this can be multi-faith in nature. Some schools also allow pupils from different religious traditions to have separate acts of worship in their own faith. Parents in Britain have the right to withdraw their children from all religious education lessons and acts of worship, but in reality very few exercise this right. It is interesting to consider why it is that in a country where an increasingly small number of people attend church regularly this should be so – and also why church schools are still very popular in many cases; even with those families who do not attend church.

- The UK has the only national parliament in the world where leaders of the established church sit by right (in the House of Lords).
- The State does not finance religious activities in the UK, but it does contribute to the upkeep of some historic church buildings. It is estimated that 30 million tourist visits are made to churches in England every year.
- Church schools are still a major provider of education in the UK – there are around 2,500 Roman Catholic and 4,700 Church of England schools.
- Religious education and daily worship of a primarily Christian nature are compulsory in state schools, but parents can withdraw their children from these if they wish.

## Major faiths in the UK

| AQA A | M1 |
| AQA B | M2 |
| EDEXCEL | M1 |
| OCR | M1 |

We will look at faiths in the UK under two groupings:

### Monotheistic religions

Christianity, Islam and Judaism all originated in the Middle East and believe in one God. They believe that humans are created by God and live one earthly life. After death they proceed to a separate spiritual life (known in Christian teaching as Heaven and Hell).

### Polytheistic religion

Hinduism, Buddhism and Sikhism originated in Asia and believe there are many gods. They also believe in re-incarnation, with no clear beginning or end to the cycle of life.

### Christianity

A very brief outline of Christianity in Great Britain covers the following points:

- There were originally two strands to Christianity in Great Britain – the Church of the Roman Empire headed by the Pope and a Celtic church (with no allegiance to Rome) found particularly in Wales, Scotland and Ireland. The continuous history of the Church of England dates from its foundation (with its base at Canterbury Cathedral) by Augustine in 597. (After the departure of the Roman legions who had occupied England and following the arrival of the Anglo-Saxons, Christianity had virtually died out in England, but the Celtic church survived. Augustine was sent by the Pope to reconvert England to Christianity. This process reduced and then ended the Celtic Christian church.)

- Throughout the Middle Ages the church in Britain remained part of the Roman Catholic church, accepting the Pope as their spiritual leader – although there were notable objectors to this such as those led by John Wycliff, an Oxford theologian and priest (died 1384).

- The Protestant Reformation of the sixteenth century was far stronger in mainland Europe than Britain. Henry VIII's decision to assert the independence of the Church of England from Roman Catholic influence in 1534 with himself (rather than the Pope) as its head, was made largely for personal and political reasons. (He wanted to divorce his first wife and remarry, but divorce was not permitted by the Roman Catholic church.) Apart from the brief reign in the sixteenth century of Queen Mary, the Roman Catholic church ceased to be the state religion in Great Britain after Henry's break – in fact, it became illegal for a British monarch to belong to the Roman Catholic church. Nevertheless, much of Ireland has always remained staunchly loyal to the Roman Catholic faith.

- In the eighteenth, and particularly the nineteenth, centuries, there was an upsurge in Protestant groups (such as Methodists and Baptists), who rejected the

The Church of England – political or religious in origin?

hierarchical basis of the traditional church and the power of the priests. Such groups placed much greater emphasis on the Bible, the Christian holy book, and less on tradition. A great religious revival swept through Wales and some of the industrial cities of England and Scotland in the early twentieth century.

In the latter part of the twentieth century there was a worldwide rise of new Christian groups or cults, and an increased popularity of groups that had originated in the United States, such as the Scientologists or the Mormons (The Church of Latter Day Saints). There are now an estimated 22,000 different Christian groups in the world, but there remains three main groupings:

- the Orthodox Church, found mainly in Eastern Europe, Russia and the Middle East
- Roman Catholic, found throughout the world, but especially in countries colonised by Spain, Portugal and France
- Protestant (or 'Free Churches') found throughout the world, but more particularly in northern Europe, northern America and those countries colonised by the English and the Dutch.

Because Christianity is now represented by so many conflicting groups it can be hard to summarise a set of 'core Christian beliefs'. However, most Christians believe that God is three beings (the Trinity) – Father, Son and Holy Spirit – but is nevertheless one God. God the Father created Heaven and Earth, but human sinfulness put a barrier between God and His creation. God then came down to Earth in the form of a human being, Jesus Christ (the Son) born of an earthly mother, to show people the way back to God. Jesus Christ suffered capital punishment at the hands of the Romans and Jews in order to overcome the power of sin, and after His death He came back to life (was resurrected), and before He returned to heaven set His followers the task of establishing Christianity. The Holy Spirit enters and lives within those who believe in Christ.

The most common act of Christian worship is a commemoration of the last meal shared by Jesus and his closest followers (his 'Disciples'), consisting of bread and wine which Jesus declared to be his body and blood. However, there is disagreement between Christian groups as to whether this was meant to be taken literally. Other disagreements exist over:

- whether the Bible is to be taken as the literal truth – or whether it is symbolic and also contains ancient folk-lore and tradition
- the power of priests and ministers of religion – whether they are direct descendants of Jesus' followers and pass on truth that has to be acknowledged, or whether they are simply the leaders in prayer and worship of their contemporary group. Some groups, especially those of a more democratic nature, base their worship almost entirely on the Bible, and the singing of hymns and communal prayers
- the role of women in the church today – St Paul (an early Christian writer who wrote a collection of books telling the young church about Jesus in the first century AD) specifically says that women do not have an active role in the leadership of the church, and Jesus chose only men to spread His message. Does this mean that women in the modern world should not be able to take a leading role – or was such action merely a reflection of where the power in society lay 2,000 years ago? The biggest single Christian group, the Roman Catholic church, is still very opposed to women priests, but many Protestant churches and the Church of England now have women priests.

## Islam

The Arabic word Islam means 'submission' – to God. The religion originated in 622 AD in Makkah (Mecca) in modern Saudi Arabia, and a pilgrimage (or 'hajj') to this

---

Is religion as much to do with politics and geography as faith?

There are now so many groups and sects who call themselves Christians that to summarise a set of basic beliefs is very difficult. You should consider whether this, in part, negates the Christian message.

Jesus Christ's birth in Palestine was said to have occurred at the time of the Roman Empire, and the modern European Calendar – with years referred to as AD (Anno Domino – Latin for the year of 'Our Lord') – is supposed to date back to the year of His birth two millennia ago.

This is perhaps one of the most important arguments in the contemporary Christian church – even if you don't go to church you should try to take a view, since it is part of the broader political argument about the role of women. In all other major religions this issue doesn't arise since all clerics are male.

holy city is still the ambition of many Muslims – the name given to followers of Islam. The Islamic religion reveres the prophet Mohammed who was the last and greatest of the prophets showing the way to God and who was born in Makkah in AD 570). Today, there are well over 1,000 million Muslims in the world, mainly in Africa, Asia and some of the southern republics of the former Soviet Union.

There is a thriving and growing Muslim population in Britain, mainly (but by no means exclusively) in families who moved to the country from the Asian sub-continent in the 1950s and 1960s. Britain's Muslim population is around one million and is still growing. There are over 600 mosques in Britain; in 1960 there were under 10. Many early mosques were founded in large existing buildings, such as redundant cinemas, but increasingly they are purpose built – adding a new and distinctive style to religious building in the UK. The mosque is not only the centre of worship, but also offers instruction in the traditional Muslim way of life as well as facilities for educational and welfare activities. The first British mosque is over 100 years old, being founded at Woking in 1890, but today's most important mosque is London's Central Mosque, with a congregation of over 5,000.

The major events of the Islamic year are the month of fasting known as Ramadan, and the festivals of Id al Fitr and Id al Adha which are marked with communal prayers. The Muslim holy book is the Qur'an.

> Try to think of the kinds of tensions that can arise in Muslim families living in multi-cultural Britain.

For some young Muslims growing up in Great Britain there can be tensions when they compare their life-style and the power of their families with those of their non-Muslim contemporaries. This can create great strain in families where the parents are trying to maintain the traditional Muslim way of life.

Although Christian theology (the understanding of the word of God) might seem predominant in Europe, it should be remembered that Spain at one time came under Islamic rule, and the first Professorship of Arabic was founded in Cambridge in 1632, followed in Oxford a few years later. Many other universities teach subjects either directly or indirectly connected with Islam. Remember, whatever your own personal beliefs, that the General Studies exam requires that you demonstrate awareness and respect for other faiths.

## Judaism

Jews were first recorded as settling in Britain at the time of the Norman Conquest. There was much anti-Semitism in the Middle Ages and beyond – in part because the Jews were seen as the people who had put Jesus to death (see 'Christianity' above), and, more pressingly, because Jews were able to lend money with interest (thus acting as the original bankers in Europe) at a time when this was considered a sin for Christians. People who could not repay their debts often sought to lay the blame on the people who had loaned them the money in the first place. The Jews have therefore been used as scapegoats by Europeans for centuries before Hitler and the Nazis. The rise of Nazism in the 1930s led to a large increase in the Jewish population of Britain, and today it stands at around 300,000 – of whom 200,000 live in London.

> Think about how Shylock, the Jewish money-lender in Shakespeare's *Merchant of Venice*, is portrayed.

The Jewish place of worship is the synagogue, where services are held on Saturdays – the Jewish 'Sabbath', or holy day. The Jewish Bible (known to Christians as the Old Testament, because it pre-dates the birth of Jesus) is divided into three sections – the Law books (the Torah), the Prophets (or Nevi'im) and the Writings (or Ketubim).

There is no single Jewish statement of faith, but one that has stood the test of time was drawn up by Maimonides, who lived in twelfth-century Spain:

1 God has, does and will create everything.
2 God is one.
3 God is not and does not have a body.

Consider these 13 points – how many would not be accepted by a Christian or a Muslim?

4  God is the first and the last.
5  It is wrong to pray to anyone or anything apart from God.
6  The words of the prophets are true.
7  The prophecy of Moses is true and he is the greatest of the prophets.
8  The Torah (Law) was given to Moses.
9  The Torah will never be changed.
10  God knows everything – everyone's thoughts and acts.
11  God rewards those who keep His commandments and punishes those who break them.
12  The Messiah will come.
13  There will be a resurrection of the dead.

The main Jewish festivals include Rosh Hashanah (New Year), Yom Kippur (Day of Atonement) and Pesach (Passover).

## Hinduism

The Hindu religion has developed over at least 4,000 years in the South Asian sub-continent. The Hindu population in Britain is about 300,000 strong – the vast majority of families having arrived between the mid-1950s and early 1970s (after which changes in immigration law make it more difficult for commonwealth citizens from Asia and Africa to establish the right to live in the UK). During the earlier part of this period most Hindus came directly from India – at a time when the British economy was in a post-war boom and labour was being sought from the countries of the former British Empire (many of whose inhabitants had been brought up to regard Britain as the 'Mother country'). However, during the 1960s the majority came from East Africa, following their expulsion from Kenya and then from Uganda. These populations were Indian in origin, having in many cases first arrived in Africa as labourers to build railways for British firms. However, many families became established in commerce, and their expulsions were based on their perceived economic power. The Jews were not the only ethnic group to be expelled from countries for what can basically be perceived as economic reasons!

The main features of Hinduism are as follows:

Hindus, as well as Jews, have been expelled from countries – but more recently.

The nature of Hindu worship is more home-based than that of many religions.

- Hindus practise their religion in their homes, where there will be a shrine with pictures or statues of deities set in a special place. There is also communal worship in temples, called 'Mandirs', where the singing of hymns ('bhajans'), accompanied by small cymbals, tambourines and other instruments is very popular. Dance can also be a form of worship – you may have seen organised dance troupes who tour communities telling the great stories of Hindu tradition in mime and dance, combining entertainment and worship. Hindus acknowledge many gods and goddesses, perhaps the best known being Krishna, Rama, Ganesh and Ambamata.

- In Hindu philosophy, there is no beginning and no end – everything goes in cycles, so there is creation, existing, declining and destruction, prior to the cycle starting again. There are two groups of sacred writing – Srti ('what has been heard') and Smrti ('remembered'). The former comes from a divine origin and has passed on orally for centuries, the latter, being remembered, contains the possibility of error, so is not so highly regarded.

The origins of Hinduism and other Asian religions are different from that of Christianity, Judaism and Islam which originated in the Middle East. In recent years, Hinduism has appealed to many western young people.

- At the heart of Hindu belief is the idea of 'Karma' (or 'destiny') – that as the human body grows old and dies, the soul will be reborn in another body (re-incarnation). The kind of body in which the soul is reborn will depend on your goodness in the previous life – good deeds leading to rebirth in a better life. Through gaining spiritual knowledge, being devout and doing good works the ultimate goal can be attained which is to break free of this cycle and be released so that the soul becomes one with the One Soul (Brahman). This state of oneness is known as 'Nirvana'.

- There are many Hindu festivals, but perhaps the best known is Diwali – the Festival of Lights, marked by the lighting of lamps. In Leicester, which probably has the largest Hindu population in the UK outside Greater London, the festival is marked by illuminations put up by the city council in the city centre. The festival is in November, and the lights remain in place to become the Christmas illuminations in December – a nice example of traditions coming together in contemporary society.

## Buddhism

'Buddhism' is a modern Western term which describes a wide range of mental and spiritual cultures that developed from the teaching of Siddhartha Gautama, the Buddha, who lived and taught in north-east India in the sixth century BC. His teachings are set out in the Tripitaka, but different schools of Buddhism have developed these, and also use other texts. The main branches of Buddhism are those found in Japan and China ('Zen'), in Tibet, Sri Lanka, Thailand and Burma.

In the 1960s Buddhism appealed to many young people who rejected Christianity.

The Buddhist Society of Great Britain and Ireland was founded in 1907, the forerunner of the present Buddhist Society founded in 1923. During the 1960s, when there was an opportunity for wider travel, many young people from Britain travelled to the Far East to discover Buddhism, which had a major impact on the Hippy Movement. It opened up a channel for spirituality for many young people who rejected their traditional upbringing of Christian worship and attending church services.

Just as in Hinduism, Buddhism contains ideas of rebirth, but Buddhists do not believe that there is a soul, or that we have any 'self' that is permanent. Buddhist teachings suggest we are a bundle of five forces – form (the body), feelings, perceptions, emotions and consciousness. It is our own desires relative to these bundles that lead them to be reincarnated and it is only when we can extinguish a desire for *all* these tendencies that 'nirvana' is reached. Since the vast majority are far from attaining this state, being reborn in a better state than in the previous life is a step along the way.

The Buddha (believed to be born in 536 BC), set out the Four Noble Truths and the Noble Eightfold Path that should be followed – these are outlined in any book about Buddhist philosophy.

## Sikhs

The Sikh religion is based on the teaching of ten 'Gurus', who were active in northern India between the fifteenth and seventeenth centuries. The first and most important of these was Guru Nanak (1469–1539). The religion is based in the Punjab in north-east India, although part of this area is now in modern-day Pakistan (which causes affront to some Sikhs, who see Punjab as their homeland).

There is a large Sikh community of over 300,000 in Britain, mainly coming originally from Punjab or from East Africa. Men's forenames are followed by the word 'Singh' meaning 'lion', and women's names by the word 'Kaur' meaning 'princess'. It is perhaps a sign of their lack of understanding of other cultures that many people in Britain think that 'Singh' is merely a surname – and never wonder why *all* Sikhs have the same name! A male Sikh is readily identified by his turban, worn to protect his uncut hair. Since this forms part of Sikh tradition, Sikh males are exempt from the requirement to wear a motor-cycle helmet, and Sikh police officers do not wear the traditional helmet, although they do have to wear a navy blue turban. This requirement for uncut hair is one of five requirements – the others being to wear a comb (to keep the hair tidy), a wrist band on the right arm, a dagger (a reminder of warrior race origins) and baggy trousers.

Sikh temples are called 'gurdwaras', and they are where most Sikhs attend regular services each Sunday. There are over 160 in Britain, cared for by elected

> Does a religion that acknowledges the holy books of other religions weaken itself – or is it a sign of tolerance?

committees, with a 'granthi' who is employed to look after the building and conduct prayers. The gurdwara serves the religious, educational, welfare and cultural needs of the Sikh community.

The Sikh scriptures are considered to be very important – worshippers prostrate themselves before them in the gurdwara. The 'message' (bani) is the source of all teaching and inspiration, coming from the ten Gurus. However, the sacred scriptures of other religions are also acknowledged, and there is a view that through meditation God can reveal Himself still – i.e. sacred books are not the end of God's words. Sikhs believe that God is present in all human beings and that the most important devotion is to meditate on Him. In common with Hindus, there is also a belief in 'Karma' and reincarnation, with each of us having an immortal soul.

**KEY POINT**

- You yourself might belong to one of the religions described above, or to another, but nevertheless we now have to acknowledge that Britain is a multi-faith community.

- There are two main strands of religions – those originating in the Middle East (Judaism, Christianity and Islam) and those originating in the Asian continent (Hinduism, Buddhism and Sikhism). The religions from the Middle East believe in one God (Monotheism), while those from Asia believe there are many gods (Polytheism).

- Judaism, Christianity and Islam believe humans live one earthly life and then proceed after death to a separate, eternal spiritual life. Hindus, Buddhists and Sikhs believe in reincarnation.

- In most religions the priests are male. Only in protestant Christianity and radical Judaism are there female priests. However, in the Church of England there are still deep splits about female priests.

- Religious activity often takes the form of commemoration of some action (such as the Last Supper in Christianity) or other communal activity – singing, praying, dancing, etc. However, there is also an important role for contemplation and meditation – particularly in Eastern religions.

- Christianity is the dominant religion in Britain, but over the past 50 years it has declined. Islam is growing in Britain, mainly because its followers have larger families rather than because people are converting to Islam.

## Progress check

1  Apart from Christianity, which is the longest-standing religious community in the UK?
2  Which religion expanded dramatically in the UK between the mid 1950s and 1970?
3  What is the role of SACRE in local education authorities?
4  Who might go on a *hajj* to Makkah?
5  The holy book of which religion is divided into the Torah, the Nevi'im and the Ketubim?
6  Which religion developed in the South Asian sub-continent over 4,000 years?
7  Who set out the Four Noble Truths?
8  What is a 'gurdwara'?

8  A Sikh temple.
7  Siddhartha Gautama, who became called 'the Buddha'.
6  Hinduism.
5  Judaism – these form the book known to Christians as the Old Testament.
4  A Muslim – it is the pilgrimage to the birthplace of the Prophet Mohammed.
3  To monitor collective worship and religious education teaching in local authority schools.
2  Islam – due to many Muslims arriving from Asia as immigrants to work in the booming British economy in the post-war years.
1  Judaism – is the next oldest religion surviving in organised form today in the UK.

# 5.2 Values

*After studying this section you should be able to:*

- *identify the factors that influence people's values*
- *distinguish between left-wing and right-wing values*
- *describe the kinds of things that lead to people altering their values.*

**LEARNING SUMMARY**

## Religious values

| | |
|---|---|
| AQA A | M1 |
| AQA B | M2 |
| EDEXCEL | M1 |
| OCR | M1 |

It is important to develop a personal viewpoint, based on evidence and thought. Think of the reasons why you have come to it and arguments that others might use to put differing views.

Some people talk as if religious values do not change, but a glance at the contemporary Christian church, for example, shows many changes in its values (although these are more pronounced in some groups than others). In Britain today many divorced people re-marry in religious ceremonies and there are homosexual and lesbian activists even among the clergy campaigning in the church. Many religious people no longer rule out abortion. This brings us to a huge moral question for believers – should religion reflect a universal truth, or should it change from age to age to reflect contemporary opinion? What, for example, about capital punishment? The Ten Commandments of Christianity and Judaism clearly state 'Thou shalt not kill', and Jesus was clear that the idea of taking 'an eye for an eye' is not acceptable – but many Christians over the centuries right up to the present day have supported the death penalty. Can wars ever be justified – it was St Thomas Aquinas, the founder of the Jesuits in the Middle Ages, who first wrote about the idea of the 'just war'. Is the use of force to overcome evil justified? Who defines evil – in World War II the battleships of both England and Germany were launched with Christian prayers. What about a Muslim 'fatwah' – a death sentence imposed by a senior Muslim cleric that any follower of Islam will be blessed for carrying out? People throughout the ages have used the name of God to justify all kinds of evil. However, many would argue that this represents an abuse of religion – which is, in itself God-given, and which followers believe will lead to eternal life.

- Religious values are usually claimed to be part of a universal truth by adherents of that faith.
- These values are usually transmitted through sacred writings, clergy and the beliefs of the faithful.
- Interpretation may change over time – or perhaps traditional teachings might be abused.
- Does this negate the concept of an 'eternal truth' in religious values?

**KEY POINT**

## Political values

| | |
|---|---|
| AQA A | M1 |
| AQA B | M1, M2 |
| EDEXCEL | M1 |
| OCR | M1 |

Such theology has always had a powerful appeal in the peasant communities of Latin America, although it has always been officially condemned by the main-stream Christian church.

Many political systems have, in fact, claimed to be based on religious values. Marxism was the first political system that clearly set out the view that the state should be atheist. Marx declared that religion was the 'opiate of the masses' – in other words, it calmed them and gave them a sense of euphoria and well-being thus stopping them from changing an unsatisfactory political system. However, just to confuse matters, there are now 'Christian Marxists' who preach 'Liberation theology' in support of poor and down-trodden people (whom they encourage to oppose their governments).

### Politics and economics

Political values are heavily influenced by the prevailing economic reality. British political views at the height of Victorian power, when the Empire was at its peak, were different to those being expressed by many in the Thatcher years in the mid-1980s, when unemployment stood at three million and Britain had become a net importer of manufactured goods for the first time since the Industrial Revolution. Many people in Britain find it hard to accept that Britain no longer exercises a role as a major power in the world. Blatant nationalism is often seen at events such as international sporting fixtures (particularly in predominantly male sports such as soccer), and this is often fanned by the tabloid press.

## Politics and the individual

Political values often deal with the relative importance of the individual in relation to that of society as a whole. In political shorthand the 'right-wing' view is the importance of freedom for individuals to act alone and achieve individual successes, and the 'left-wing' view (in its most extreme form) would be that the individual is merely part of a broader society, and the ultimate well-being of society as a whole is the goal to aim for. The reality is that, in democratic countries, there is now less stress on idealism and more on pragmatism – the idea of finding the best solution for the immediate problem. Britain has therefore seen a Conservative government increase spending on the National Health Service (even if the circumstances were sometimes rather controversial) and the Labour government encouraging the development of private enterprise and share-owning.

There are a series of questions you could ask yourself in order to identify your own political stance, such as:

A Do you think people succeed primarily through their own efforts?

B Are some people privileged by birth or education?

C Should everybody have the same educational experience, based at a local community school?

D Should people who have the money be able to spend it on providing things like private health care and education for their children?

E Is it right that the profits made by an industry should be passed on to the shareholders rather than to its workers?

F Are the poorest in society best helped by allowing successful wealth creators to be successful on behalf of the country as a whole?

> **KEY POINT**
> Many political systems claim to be based on religious roots; only Marxism began as an entirely atheist philosophy.

*Western democracies seek the 'middle way' – democracies rarely take extreme views, because electors can easily reject them.*

*If you answered 'yes' to questions A, B, E and F your views tend towards a right-wing, conservative perspective, in which the role of government is minimised and the rights of the individual rather than those of society as a whole predominate. If you said 'yes' to B and C you tend towards a more radical (the word 'socialist' seems out of fashion) approach. Of course, 'no' answers reverse these answers.*

## Social values

| AQA A | M1 |
| AQA B | M2 |
| EDEXCEL | M1 |
| OCR | M1 |

### Sexual behaviour

We hear a lot about a decline in social values, and by this people are often referring to sexual behaviour, viewing it in the context of their particular religious values. Different religions provide different outlooks – in Islamic law a woman found guilty of adultery can be stoned to death, while according to the Christian Bible this 'sin' can lead to eternal damnation unless repented of.

Values relating to sexual behaviour have changed radically in the past century.

- Victorian morality put women (or more precisely, wives) on a pedestal – while at the same time Victorian cities contained many more prostitutes than nowadays and 'respectable' middle-class married men thought nothing of visiting them.

- During the 1960s a 'sexual revolution' took place. This era was known as the 'Swinging Sixties' and is associated with more liberal attitudes towards sex. (However, it should be remembered that abortion wasn't 'legalised' until 1967 and contraception for single women was still quite difficult to obtain.) There are two opposing viewpoints on whether this was a good thing – one saying that this led to a spread of promiscuity, pornography, abortion and sexually transmitted disease and another saying that relationships became more honest, that sexual

*Are we now more honest and open or is current sexual behaviour a recipe for social disaster?*

liberation led to more people (particularly women) escaping repressive relationships and gaining pleasure, and that sex was no longer regarded as 'dirty' and concerned with reproduction rather than personal fulfilment.

## Influences on social values

There are various sources that contribute to the formation of our values:

### Religion

Many people claim that our values have divine origins. We find them in our holy writings, whatever religion we belong to, and these reflect the 'divine view' of what is right. So, for example, for Christians the Bible is full of statements about values. These are, however, sometimes contradictory – we are told that it is easier for a camel to pass through the eye of a needle than for a rich person to get into heaven, but in another passage we are told in the 'parable (story) of the talents' that the father of the family (alluding to God) rewarded the son who made the best investment and the biggest profit. Although people who belong to a religious group find it provides a basis for many of their values, this basis is not necessarily a binding one if immediate pressures make the values of the group difficult to accept (the attitudes of many European and North American Catholic women towards the use of contraception might be seen as one example here).

### The family

Another major source of social values is our immediate family, which for a majority means our parent or parents. From our earliest childhood we learn attitudes of good and bad, right and wrong, from our immediate household. Since these values go back to our earliest days, and are bound up with the provision of love, warmth, comfort and food that is vital to us all, they are extremely powerful. We also learn a lot from the environment in which we live – the immediate family provides primary socialisation and our broader environment gives us secondary socialisation. Thus someone brought up in a community of high-rise flats with high levels of unemployment, low educational expectations and high social breakdown will hold different values to one brought up on a landed estate with high levels of income, a public school education and a high expectation of future success.

### Popular culture

Often boosted by the power of today's mass media, many people (especially the younger generation) adopt what are sometimes seen as 'popular values'. Pop stars and sports personalities are often seen as role models and their views adopted by fans – although this may not be permanent since stardom is often short-lived. We see, for example, great fear expressed by some parents and older people over the spread of a drug culture through pop music and culture, but on the other hand the 'Kick racism out of soccer' campaign has had a very positive effect in promoting social equality among the younger generation. We are also seeing the rise of quite young and socially influential business leaders who have a strong impact on people's views, for example:

- Richard Branson campaigning for easily available contraception
- Anita Roddick, the founder of Body Shop, a prominent campaigner against animal testing in the cosmetics industry.

**KEY POINT**

- Many people talk about a decline in 'social values' when what they are really talking about is a more liberal view of sexual relationships.
- 'Victorian morality' was often quite hypocritical, particularly in the way in which women (especially prostitutes) were regarded.
- People who are members of a religious faith usually believe that social values are God given and set out in holy books such as the Bible.
- Arguably, the strongest influences on our values are our immediate family and community – a process known as 'socialisation'.

## Progress check

1 Name one religious ceremony that might take place in some Christian churches today that would not have been possible in 1900.

2 Which was the first political theory to expressly support atheism?

3 How would a 'right wing' political supporter view the power of the individual in society?

4 In which recent decade did what people talk about as a 'sexual revolution' occur?

5 What is the name often given to the process of learning who we are, and our role in society from our immediate family?

5 'Primary' socialisation – as opposed to 'secondary', which is what we learn from our broader community.
4 The 1960s.
3 The power of the individual is paramount, and overrides the collective view of society. (Mrs Thatcher once famously said 'There is no longer such a thing as "society".')
2 Communism – as first expressed in Karl Marx's *Communist Manifesto* published in 1848.
1 The re-marriage of previously divorced people is one example.

# 5.3 Morals

**After studying this section you should be able to:**

- outline factors that help determine our moral judgements
- express your views on a variety of contemporary moral issues

LEARNING SUMMARY

## Bases for moral judgements

| | |
|---|---|
| AQA A | M1 |
| AQA B | M2 |
| EDEXCEL | M1 |
| OCR | M1 |

The terms 'morals' and 'values' are often used interchangeably. If we were forced to distinguish between them we might say that 'morals' are directly concerned with how we behave, while 'values' are more of a philosophy about what is right and wrong.

Sometimes we might make judgements, or act in a certain way because we believe that we are told to do that by some higher authority – for example, a holy book, or the sayings of a guru or a prophet. Our parents and close family are another means through which a sense of right and wrong are instilled in us (we are told off for doing some things and praised for others). We come to conform to what is expected of us, but there is more to this than merely the kind of training you would give a pet dog.

As humans we expect to be given reasons for acting or behaving in a certain way – among young children you will frequently hear the question 'Why?'. As children get older their parents often say in relation to an action considered to be wrong 'What if everybody did that?', suggesting that this would be a bad thing. Later on they might say to a teenager with increasing sophistication of thought, 'How would you feel if somebody did that to you?' This is more complicated because you have to consider both whether you would like to be treated like that, and also whether this in itself counts as a reason for not doing it to *somebody else*.

Conscience affects our behaviour.

When we are confronted with a moral dilemma, and, for example, have to discriminate good from bad, we should be able to give reasons for our decisions. Just because we like something it is not in itself enough for saying it is good – that is merely a statement of personal preference. Moral judgements affect the way we think and act in the world that we live in. Different people will come to different conclusions – often deeply held. Your views will reflect your background, both in your immediate family and in the predominant culture in which you have been brought up.

Moral judgements are more serious than matters of pure choice – they affect the way we see the world.

> 'Morals' relate to our perception of rightness and wrongness in human behaviour. A 'moral person' is seen as one who has, or who teaches, high standards of behaviour – and may be seen as 'virtuous'.

**KEY POINT**

## Progress check

1 Name three sources from which we get our views of what is right and wrong.

2 How does our conscience help to shape our attitudes?

3 Give three examples of moral dilemmas in contemporary society, which lead to people holding deeply opposing views.

3 Sexual behaviour; abortion; genetic engineering; war; animal rights; euthanasia; and whether it is ever right to break the law – you might well be able to think of others.

2 Because it makes us consider the consequences of an action – whether, for example, it will cause pleasure or pain to somebody else.

1 Possible sources include:
Religious beliefs or writings, our close family, the community in which we grow up (e.g. think of the divide between Catholic and Protestant communities in Northern Ireland).

## Sample question and model answer

The views of Mary Whitehouse.

'Men, women and children listen and view [radio and TV] at risk of serious damage to their morals, their patriotism, their discipline and their family.'

*(Mary Whitehouse)*

To what extent do you think the values of a decent society are undermined by what is seen and heard on the TV and radio?

**Stage 1**
Introduction.

- *Mary Whitehouse rose to prominence in the 1970s by complaining about the amount of swearing and bad language on TV.*
- *This broadened out to consider what she regarded as violence, corruption and anti-religious bias in the British media as a whole.*
- *The National Viewers and Listeners Association that she formed became a powerful, conservative force, particularly in the period 1964–80, when it saw itself as a bastion against 'progressiveness', including sex, violence and blasphemy in the media.*

**Stage 2**
Arguments to support the assertion.

- *Now put the case in support of Mary Whitehouse's view as objectively and dispassionately as you can.*
- *You might mention the fact that depictions of violence, sex and the treatment of women in a derogatory manner all became increasingly common in the media.*
- *At the same time suicides, abortion, pregnancy outside marriage and numbers going to prison all rose sharply.*
- *Young people became increasingly cynical about party politics and there was a decline in the percentage of people who voted in elections.*
- *Crime has increased, and in some cities ghetto areas now exist.*
- *Traditional family life – husband, wife and children – is no longer a reality for very many.*

**Stage 3**
Now consider the counter-arguments.

- *The media can be a source of enlightenment and education – people have a free choice over what to watch.*
- Social *breakdown is caused by social factors – unemployment, poor housing, low educational attainment, etc. – not by watching TV.*
- *The media are often a catharsis for people who lead drab lives – there is no firm evidence that it causes damage to the morals of people who watch or listen.*
- *The BBC charter suggests that the media can play an inspirational role, 'Nation shall speak peace unto nation'.*

## Sample question and model answer

**Stage 4**
Draw your own conclusion, coming to a firm viewpoint.

Ensure your conclusion comes from points raised earlier in your answer.

- If there is a more open view towards sex, politics, etc., this is merely reflecting the society in which we live, it is not *causing* the changes.
- After considering both sides of the argument, and acknowledging that both have adherents, try to summarise the key 'battlegrounds' within the points you have made.
- State your personal view – examiners will reward a strong conclusion which is based on the arguments advanced, so do not hold back from being firm.

*An example of a conclusion is as follows:*

There is no clear evidence that radio and, especially, television undermine the value of society. I believe that these are primarily forms of entertainment, and that the cruel realities of many people's daily lives – unemployment, failed education, poor housing and social breakdown – are far greater factors. There is a basic arrogance in the position taken by middle-class zealots like Mary Whitehouse – that she can watch programmes in order to denounce them for having an effect on others. I have heard this expressed as, 'This will not corrupt me, it may corrupt you, it will certainly corrupt them'. There is no firm evidence to support this and in my view the values of society have actually been undermined by far more tangible factors than those of channels of entertainment.

## Practice examination questions

### Short answer questions

1 What influence has religion had in the British education system?

2 What are the three main groups found within Christianity in the world?

3 What is meant by 'right' and 'left' in politics?

### Essay question

4 To what extent do religious values form the basis of political and social values?

# Chapter 6

# Creativity and innovation

- Twentieth-century literature
- Twentieth-century music
- Twentieth-century architecture

## 6.1 Twentieth-century literature

After studying this section you should be able to:

- identify some of the milestones in literature of the twentieth century
- name various British war poets of World War I and cite some of their works

### Important literature of the twentieth century

| | |
|---|---|
| AQA A | M1 |
| AQA B | M1, M2 |
| EDEXCEL | M1 |
| OCR | M1 |

Some books are written for entertainment, others in order to get a political message across – make sure you give examples of different genres.

There has been a wide variety of literature written over the last 100 years but in terms of General Studies, pieces which prompt discussion are those which have a profound effect on the thinking of their day – for example, the British war poets, who had great impact during the post World War I period. We will look at them in more detail in a separate section.

Important books of the twentieth century range from children's classics, to political allegory; from books originally considered obscene, to feminist classics. No doubt you will be able to add to the list provided in Table 6.1 particularly with titles from the latter part of the century with which you might be more familiar from your personal reading.

'Anthropomorphism' is the giving of human characteristics to animals, gods or other non-human objects. Another example in literature is in George Orwell's *Animal Farm*.

*Table 6.1 Important books of the twentieth century*

| Year | Author | Title | Notes |
|------|--------|-------|-------|
| 1902 | Beatrix Potter | *The Tale of Peter Rabbit* | Animals as people (anthropomorphism) |
| 1904 | J.M. Barrie | *Peter Pan* | All royalties still go to the Great Ormond Street Children's Hospital |
| 1904 | Anton Checkov | *The Cherry Orchard* | A play popular in its original Russian and when translated into English |
| 1908 | Kenneth Grahame | *The Wind in the Willows* | Again, animals as people |
| 1913 | D.H. Lawrence | *Sons and Lovers* | When first published, this was declared obscene and all copies destroyed |
| 1915 | D.H. Lawrence | *The Rainbow* | |
| 1920 | Agatha Christie | *The Mysterious Affair at Styles* | Her first novel – introduced Hercule Poirot. Reflected post-war escapism |
| 1922 | James Joyce | *Ulysses* | This was a major step forward in the development of the novel |
| 1926 | A.A. Milne | *Winnie the Pooh* | More animals as people! |
| 1929 | Ernest Hemingway | *A Farewell to Arms* | Powerful political writing |
| 1929 | Robert Graves | *Goodbye to All That* | Autobiographical experiences of World War I |
| 1929 | W.H. Auden | *Poems* (his first collection of poetry) | Major influence on poetry of the century |
| 1932 | Aldous Huxley | *Brave New World* | Science fiction which gave warnings for future societies |
| 1933 | Vera Brittain | *Testament of Youth* | World War I from a woman's perspective |
| 1937 | J.R.R. Tolkein | *The Hobbit* | |
| 1945 | George Orwell | *Animal Farm* | Satire on the development of the Soviet Union |
| 1947 | Tennessee Williams | *A Streetcar Named Desire* | Has been called the 'best play ever written by an American'. |

| Year | Author | Title | Notes |
|------|--------|-------|-------|
| 1948 | George Orwell | *1984* | Originally titled 'The Last Man in Europe' – this was a warning about the dangers of dictatorship |
| 1949 | Simone de Beauvoir | *The Second Sex* | One of the classic texts of modern Feminism |
| 1953 | Arthur Miller | *The Crucible* | Allegorical denunciation of the McCarthy purges in the USA |
| 1956 | John Osborne | *Look Back in Anger* | This play is about one of the original 'Angry Young Men' |
| 1957 | Boris Pasternak | *Dr Zhivago* | |
| 1958 | Harold Pinter | *The Birthday Party* | |
| 1960 | Stan Barstow | *A Kind of Loving* | One of the first writers to popularise novels on the brutality of working-class life |
| 1967 | Nell Dunn | *Poor Cow* | Female writer about working-class reality |
| 1967 | P.D. James | *Unnatural Causes* | Detective stories have remained popular throughout the century |

## The war poets

| | |
|---|---|
| AQA A | M1 |
| AQA B | M1, M2 |
| EDEXCEL | M1 |
| OCR | M1 |

If you know any of this poetry, you might be able to apply it to any discussion of conflict in a General Studies exam.

Owen and Sassoon give the most direct descriptions of their experiences of war.

There can be few better examples of writing having a profound effect on the consciousness of succeeding generations than that of the group of poets who described the horrors they experienced while serving as soldiers in World War I. Much of what they wrote can be applied to all human conflicts – which in part explains their continuing power in describing what one of the poets, Wilfred Owen, called 'the pity of war'.

Owen went to France in 1913 where he taught English until he enlisted for the army in 1915. He was an officer at the Battle of the Somme in 1916, and a year later he was hospitalised with shell-shock. In hospital he met Siegfried Sassoon, who worked with him on developing his writing. He then returned to fight in France and died one week before the end of the war. He was awarded the Military Cross posthumously but only four of his poems were published during his life. Full recognition came later and the composer Benjamin Britten used nine of the war poems in his *War Requiem* (1962). Owen is now perhaps the best-known poet of World War I and one of his best-known poems is 'Strange Meeting'.

Siegfried Sassoon lived a rather happy-go-lucky life up to the age of 28, failing to complete his degree at Cambridge. He joined the army on the first day of the war, and this changed his life. At the start he was enthusiastic and was awarded the Military Cross (a medal which he later threw into the River Mersey). However, his experiences in the trenches turned him into a pacifist. He got into a situation where he was about to be court martialled, but his friend Robert Graves persuaded him to claim shell shock and enter hospital (where he met Owen). He then decided that his place was alongside the men he led and he returned to the Front. However, he was injured by being shot in the head by one of his own men in July 1918. He then took no further part in the war. His early poems talk of the qualities that war brings out in men, but later he wrote only of the bitterness and horror of war. One of his most famous poems is called 'How to die'. He also compared the lives of the soldiers with those who controlled the war – the latter 'guzzling and gulping in the best hotel'. After the war he became involved in pacifist politics and died aged 81.

Robert Graves was a classical scholar and poet. His first volume of poetry (published in 1917 and entitled *Fairies and Fusiliers*) recounts his war experiences, but he is perhaps best known for his satirical military memoir published in novel form in 1929 entitled *Goodbye To All That*. Graves went on to hold several university professorships after the war and moved to Majorca in 1929.

Another famous war poet was Rupert Brook. He was posted with the Royal Naval Division in 1915 to the Dardanelles and died (whilst not on active service) of blood poisoning in Greece aged 28. Shortly before his death his book *1914 and Other*

*Poems* was published which showed a rather romantic patriotism. However, in letters and other writings that were published after his death his views on the tragedy and waste of war is made plain.

> The messages of the War Poets are political as well as artistic and can be used with good effect in many arguments on the rights and wrongs of military conflict, etc.

**KEY POINT**

# 6.2 Twentieth-century music

*After studying this section you should be able to:*

**LEARNING SUMMARY**

- *give examples of different forms of music that have been popular in the twentieth century*
- *cite some key musical works of the twentieth century*

## Classical music

| AQA A | M1 |
| AQA B | M1 |
| EDEXCEL | M1 |
| OCR | M1 |

Music, just like writing, can convey broader messages that are often very powerful.

Just as is the case with literature, music is not just a source of entertainment: it can also at times carry social or political messages that affect many people who listen to it. In classical music, one of the most popular pieces of the last century was 'The Planet Suite' by Gustav Holst – a series of musical pieces written in 1916 and reflecting the characteristics of the gods after whom the planets are named. The often discordant and staccato 'Mars' reflects the newly mechanised horror of World War I (when tanks were first used), while 'Jupiter' is depicted in an upbeat, jolly music – one theme of which was later used for the hymn and nationalistic song 'I Vow To Thee My Country'.

## Jazz

| AQA A | M1 |
| AQA B | M1 |
| EDEXCEL | M1 |
| OCR | M1 |

If you write about pop music in an exam, treat it with the seriousness it deserves as a modern musical art form.

Jazz was a form of music that caught the popular mood in the years after World War I, when it developed around Chicago. This kind of music was almost exclusively played by Black musicians, and many bands and musicians went on to achieve world-wide fame – for example, Louis 'Satchmo' Armstrong. However, although music played by Black musicians was very popular, in social terms it did very little to further social equality between Blacks and Whites. Indeed, when pop-music eventually emerged as a form in its own right, the rock and roll that had developed from jazz was rejected by some as 'nigger music'. White singers like Elvis Presley in the 1950s were condemned for this, just as much as for his physical gyrations – which were denounced as being 'lewd'.

Pop developed in its own right, particularly after the 1960s when British groups like The Beatles and The Rolling Stones, and US groups like The Beach Boys and singers such as Bob Dylan, elevated pop to a level some now consider to be a serious art form.

## Musicals

| AQA A | M1 |
| AQA B | M1 |
| EDEXCEL | M1 |
| OCR | M1 |

The musical has often, but not always, been a form of escapist entertainment.

Another form of music that has been popular since the 1920s has been the musical. Perfected as an art form by Rogers and Hammerstein in the 1940s, musical shows provided an escapist glamour and glitz in a time of hardship and deprivation. However, by the 1960s the spectacle had been replaced by serious, even sombre themes. A classic work of this latter period was 'Hair' – a tribute to Hippies who resisted the call-up for the Vietnam War and which for a generation of young people on both sides of the Atlantic represented a powerful political message using a Pop medium (as well as providing a first glimpse of stage nudity). In Britain since the early 1980s, declining social and economic prosperity saw a return to lavish escapism, particularly in the works of people like Sir Andrew Lloyd-Webber (e.g. *Cats* in 1982, *Phantom of the Opera* in 1988). Such works proved enormously popular and led to continued popularity for musicals during the 1990s (for example, *Les Miserables* and *Miss Saigon*).

## Dance

| | |
|---|---|
| AQA A | M1 |
| AQA B | M1 |
| EDEXCEL | M1 |
| OCR | M1 |

Ballet is another art form popular throughout the twentieth century, and often causing political controversy – for example, the composer Stravinsky leaving Russia in 1914 and, more recently, the New Labour Government giving National Lottery money (largely provided by less well-off people in society) to support ballet, which many see as an elitist art form. Emerging from the ballet tradition has come **Modern Dance** – perhaps most notably demonstrated in the UK by the 'Ballet Rambert'.

Table 6.2 provides a summary of some of the key pieces of music during the twentieth century.

*Table 6.2 Important milestones in music during the twentieth century*

These dates, as with the literary highlights in Table 6.1, concentrate on the earlier part of the century. Use your own knowledge to add more recent events and musicians, etc. to the list – e.g. Bob Geldof and Live Aid (1985)

| Year | Composer | Title | Notes |
|---|---|---|---|
| 1910 | Igor Stravinsky | *The Firebird* | Radical ballet music |
| 1916 | Gustav Holst | *The Planet Suite* | |
| 1920s | | *The Charleston* and *The Black Bottom* | In the 'Roaring '20s' many young people pushed at the accepted styles of fashion, music and entertainment. Dances like the Charleston scandalised society – as did the short dresses and 'swing music' now popular |
| 1930 | Edith Piaf | many | French singer, first appeared in cabaret |
| 1935 | George Gershwin | *Porgy and Bess* | The first opera written for a cast of Black actors |
| 1935 | Fred Astaire | *Top Hat* | The film that became synonymous with Ginger Rogers and with dance routines |
| 1936 | Sergei Prokofiev | *Peter and the Wolf* | Soviet composer who went on to world acclaim |
| 1948 | Cole Porter | *Kiss Me Kate* | Classic musical based on Shakespeare's play *Taming of the Shrew* |
| 1950s | Pop music emerges from the music of American Blacks | | |
| 1962 | Paul McCartney/ John Lennon | *Love Me Do/ She Loves You*, etc. | The birth of a new era |

## Progress check

1  'Mars, the Bringer of War' (which looks to the mechanised horror of wars to come) is one of the pieces in which musical work?

2  What type of music became very popular in the years after World War I?

3  Give two reasons why many criticised the young Elvis Presley when he first shot to fame as a rock and roll singer?

4  For what style of music did Rogers and Hammerstein achieve fame?

5  Name the Russian composer of ballet works such as 'The Firebird'.

5 Igor Stravinsky.
4 The musical.
3 Because he was a white singer who performed 'nigger music' and because of his body gyrations which were seen as lewd and corrupting!
2 Jazz.
1 'The Planet Suite' by Gustav Holst.

# 6.3 Twentieth-century architecture

- *give examples of how architecture impacts upon society*
- *briefly outline the history of architectural development in the twentieth century.*

## The influence of architecture on society

AQA A    M1
AQA B    M3
EDEXCEL  M1
OCR      M1

Styles in architecture affect both domestic dwellings that we live in and other buildings great and small that we see around us. Architecture affects each one of us in a very personal way and can be examined at different levels, such as the aesthetic (which is what this chapter is looking at) or the sociological (for example, the effects of living in some of the huge municipal housing estates that were built mainly in the 1950s and 1960s).

> You should be able to look at the development of one of the forms of the Arts, including architecture, found in this chapter and argue a personal case for the merits of the chosen form.
>
> **KEY POINT**

Dramatic changes, mirrored in society at large, have taken place in architectural style. Today's buildings use materials that were not even invented 100 years ago.

Important features of the changing face of architecture in the twentieth century are:

- buildings today feature mass production rather than individual craftsmanship
- architects of great buildings now have new masters – no longer is it mainly government, local councils and wealthy patrons commissioning buildings; today the great buildings are those commissioned by international corporations
- the twentieth century saw the development of 'housing for all' and of 'amenity complexes' such as huge shopping or leisure complexes (increasingly situated away from town centres as more and more people own cars).

There are well-known examples of large indoor shopping centres – e.g. Meadowhall in Sheffield – but try to think of any local developments in your area.

Industrialisation in the nineteenth century led to the need for new kinds of buildings, and then the rapid growth of towns led to the pressure to build upwards (i.e. blocks of flats). Politics has always influenced building and architecture, with the growth of socialism leading to a belief that everyone had a right to decent standards of accommodation, for example.

Architecture is not only about houses and commercial buildings. Think also of modern church design, such as Coventry Cathedral, or the Roman Catholic cathedral in Liverpool. Do you have any other local examples?

### Changes in building materials

Technological developments led to dramatic changes in construction and led to huge visual differences. Perhaps most notable was the development of the steel-framed building which meant that:

- walls no longer took the weight of the building, so could be more decorative, or could give way to much larger areas of glass
- buildings could go much higher, wrapped safely round their metal frame.

The invention of the lift by Otis in the 1890s also meant that the height of a building was no longer limited by how many stairs its occupants could climb. Reinforced concrete became a popular building material: because it was cheaper and more flexible, it allowed greater variation in design.

> Aesthetics and technological developments combined to create many of the striking buildings of the last century, which got higher and higher as the century progressed – culminating in buildings such as the Sears Tower – and used increasing amounts of glass.
>
> **KEY POINT**

## Notable styles and architects of the modern era

AQA A ▶ M1
AQA B ▶ M3
EDEXCEL ▶ M1
OCR ▶ M1

Until the latter part of the nineteenth century buildings were mainly historical in style – for example, some of the great municipal Town Halls used columns to support them that could have come from Ancient Greece. In the twentieth century styles changed and owed less to historical styles.

### Art Nouveau

This style became popular at the very end of the 1800s and in the years up to the start of World War I. As a style it tried to cut links with the past, and used long, curving lines – often based on sinuous plant forms, with a strong element of fantasy. The best surviving examples are probably the entrances to many of the Paris metro stations. The style, both in architecture and in pure art, helped pave the way for modern architecture and art. Charles Rennie Mackintosh is the best remembered British architect of the style – his Glasgow Art School (1898) is still considered a masterpiece of Art Nouveau.

> Architectural developments in the early twentieth century were a clear attempt to break links with the past – why do you think this was the case?

This style – which has enjoyed something of a revival in prints and paintings, particularly among the young in recent years – tended to become over-elaborate. Furthermore, since the style was individualistic, it was not suited to mass production, and became increasingly expensive. Art Nouveau failed to outlive World War I as a popular form of architecture.

### Art Deco

> In a General Studies exam you should be able to combine a description of the functional use of a building with its artistic aesthetic merits.

Skyscrapers first appeared in the United States at the end of the 1800s – the first being the Wainwright Building in St Louis (1890–91). The Chicago School of Architects set out to erect high buildings (helped by steel framing and the lift, as mentioned above). These buildings often contained elements of Art Deco – the decorative style that followed the demise of Art Nouveau. Classic examples of Art Deco, known the world over, are:

- the Chrysler Building (1930)
- the Empire State Building (1931), 381 metres high and perhaps immortalised in the film 'King Kong' in the 1930s.

### The Bauhaus

This movement comprised a group of mainly German architects and designers. Based in Weimar in 1919, it moved to Dessau in 1926. The main features of it were that:

- it was founded by Walter Gropius, who was increasingly hounded by the Nazis in the 1930s, and eventually forced out of Germany. He then moved to the US to carry on his work
- the style used increasing amounts of steel, glass and concrete, seeking to exploit mass production materials
- in the late 1920s social responsibility became important to the school – they demonstrated low-cost housing in Berlin and Frankfurt and developed cheap and popular house contents, such as chairs made from plywood
- in 1932 a book called *The International Style* led to the naming of this type of design being popularised at the Bauhaus as 'International'

> The Bauhaus is a sad example of how politics can work against art – you might be able to use such an example at several points in a General Studies exam.

- the Nazis hated the ideals of those working at the Bauhaus – they considered them to be left-wing radicals. In 1932 the Bauhaus buildings were ransacked with covert Nazi support. The group tried to start again in a disused factory in Berlin, but this was raided by the police and then closed for good
- the leaders of the Bauhaus joined the exodus of artists and intellectuals from

Nazi Germany as Europe slid towards war in the 1930s – this provides a sad example of how an attempt to show social responsibility can become entwined and strangled by the evil of Fascism.

## Modernism

This was another style popularised in the 1930s. Sometimes looking quite stark and brutal, the style made frequent use of modern methods and the use of materials such as reinforced concrete. This enabled the construction of quick, cheap housing which was much needed at the time.

- Le Corbusier is the best-known exponent of this style. Born Charles-Edouard Jeanneret (1887–1965), some of his fantastic schemes still capture the imagination of people to this day.
- He urged that people should abandon traditional cities and move out to fantastic skyscrapers, regimentally built in vast parks.
- His dream was never realised (perhaps *could never* be realised), but smaller scale examples of his work survive to this day, sometimes mentioned in the more trendy travel books, such as the *Rough Guides*. A good example of Le Corbusier's work can be found in working-class housing in large blocks of flats in Vienna.

## Post-modernism

This style flourished from the mid-1960s, in part as a reaction to 'brutalism' in design and the large-scale use of concrete in buildings. Post-modernist buildings began to take on a flamboyance, looking light and airy – and sometimes so open that infrastructure pipework and ducts are all exposed to the eye. Examples of this style are:

- the Pompidou Centre designed by Richard Rogers (an English architect). This is the arts centre in Paris that opened in 1977, and which is constructed in steel and glass.
- The A T and T Building in New York (1984) is another good example – with its Greek-style pediment to top the building.
- A good, recent example in London is Canary Wharf and, just over the river, The Dome built to celebrate the new millennium.

## Restoration

Not all architecture is about creating brand new buildings – what advantages are there in re-cycling existing buildings?

This style has also proved popular in the years since the 1970s. You can probably think of examples of large buildings that have been transformed for new and current use. A good example that will be known to many young people will be the chain of Weatherspoon pubs, often created within the shells of buildings that had previously been banks, cinemas or had a range of other uses.

There are also some good examples of new buildings constructed in the style of historic buildings, perhaps none better than The Globe Theatre – the reconstruction of Shakespeare's original theatre on London's South Bank.

> Some important developments in architectural style over the last 100 years are as follows:
> - After World War I few could afford large individually designed, traditional country houses.
> - There was a need to build decent houses for many people and with prefabricating and new versatile materials such as reinforced concrete, this became possible.
> - Some designers and architects showed that the provision of mass housing could also demonstrate an aesthetic awareness – e.g. the Bauhaus group and the work of Le Corbusier.

KEY POINT

- In the latter part of the twentieth century there was a reaction to what was seen as the 'brutalism' of buildings containing concrete and prefabricated parts, so some outstanding buildings from the time use lots of glass and stainless steel, e.g. Richard Rogers' Pompidou Centre in Paris.
- Today the restoration, or recreation, of older buildings (often put to new uses), is popular – perhaps a romantic desire to look back to an earlier generation? The Globe Theatre in London (the recreation of Shakespeare's original sixteenth-century theatre) is a good contemporary example.

## Progress check

1 What notable development in building technology meant that walls no longer had to hold the weight of the building?

2 What invention by Otis meant that buildings could in future be realistically built to much greater heights?

3 What flamboyant style of art, popular in the early years of the twentieth century, is reflected in many of the entrances and buildings of the Paris metro?

4 What name was given to the group of mainly German architects and designers originally based in Weimar in 1919, and moving to Dessau in 1926?

5 By what name is the visionary designer and architect Charles-Edouard Jeanneret better known?

6 Name the architectural movement that flourished from the mid-1960s that sought to move to a more light, airy and flamboyant style.

7 Who was the British architect who designed the Pompidou Centre in Paris?

1 Steel frames.
2 The lift ('elevator' in American).
3 Art Nouveau.
4 The Bauhaus.
5 Le Corbusier.
6 Post-modernism.
7 Richard Rogers.

## Sample question and model answer

How have technological advances enabled architects to be increasingly creative in their designs for buildings over the last century?

**Step 1**
Before you begin writing you might find a few minutes brain-storming is productive:

*Example of a brainstorm:*

CIVIC/PUBLIC
– often built to demonstrate a progressive usage
– good example – Pompidou Centre

DOMESTIC
Houses      Flats
materials    height
              lifts
              prefabrication

MODERN BUILDINGS

RELIGIOUS
reflects style of worship
as well as materials available

COMMERCIAL
must fit purpose;
use of steel, concrete, glass

**Step 2**
Short introduction – the examiner is only looking for some context.

- *Define the areas you have chosen to explore – for example:*

Over the last hundred years the styles of many types of buildings have changed. An examination of domestic, commercial, religious and public buildings will reveal that the developments in architectural styles owe much to technology as well as to artistic innovation.

## Sample question and model answer *(continued)*

**Step 3**
Set out the major
technological developments

**Step 4**
Apply this to specific
buildings – remember you
will gain marks for this, and
for giving some personal
perspective on
how successful the
architects have been.

If you get side-tracked you
will not actually lose any
marks, but you will have less
time for relevant points or
making a valid argument.

**Step 5**
Conclusion.

*Describe and assess the importance of major technological advances – particularly:*

- *steel framing at the heart of buildings*
- *use of materials such as glass and concrete*
- *the use of inventions like lifts and air conditioning.*

*Analyse **how** such innovations have been of help to architects.*

- *Think of exciting examples of buildings constructed over the past century, e.g.*
  - *the Empire State Building*
  - *the AT & T Building*
  - *the Pompidou Centre*
  - *the Roman Catholic cathedral in Liverpool.*
- *You might also refer directly to good local examples known to you – this helps to show the examiner you are applying what you have learned to your own personal experience.*
- *Show how the technological developments you have outlined have helped create a striking and creative design.*
- *Resist the temptation to 'knock' modern architecture – it is not relevant to this question.*
- *Just as with your introduction, be brief and succinct, while at the same time being relevant; show the examiner you know about this topic, e.g.*

'The last century has seen a revolution in building design. In part this reflects changing artistic taste, and in a world of such rapid advance it is perhaps not surprising that much that is traditional has fallen from grace and fashion. However, the style, size and complexity of many modern buildings, including those referred to in this essay, would simply not have been achievable if it had not been for technological advances. It is clear that the technologist and the architect together have been responsible for the creation of the many stirring and innovative buildings we see around us today.

## Practice examination questions

### Short answer questions

**1**  What technological advances in building techniques affected building styles from the latter years of the 1800s?

**2**  What was George Orwell's message in *Animal Farm* and why did he use animals to get the message across?

**3**  How has the Musical changed and developed in format from the 1930s to the present day?

### Essay question

**4**  It has been said that our buildings help shape our lives. Discuss and give examples of buildings known to you that help explain what is meant by this statement.

# Chapter 7

# Media and communication

*The following topics are covered in this chapter:*

- *The power and influence of the Press*
- *Television – 'the box in the corner'*

## 7.1 The power and influence of the Press

*After studying this section you should be able to:*

- *compare the contrasting styles of tabloid and broadsheet newspapers*
- *describe means used by the Press to influence us*
- *consider arguments for and against greater control over newspapers*

**LEARNING SUMMARY**

### Tabloid and broadsheet newspapers

| | |
|---|---|
| AQA A | M1 |
| AQA B | M1, M2 |
| EDEXCEL | M1 |
| OCR | M1 |

A large majority of British adults will look at a newspaper every day. Newspapers are sometimes described as 'heavy' or 'light', depending on the extent to which the news and articles in them are an analysis of political, social, economic or scientific concerns, or feature more 'human concern' stories (often about people who are in the entertainment or sports industries, or otherwise in the public eye). Newspapers are also categorised as 'broadsheet' or 'tabloid' – originally terms referring to the size of the paper, but today also including an analysis of their content.

Examples of tabloid newspapers include:

| | |
|---|---|
| *The Sun* | *The Express* |
| *The Mirror* | *Daily Star* |
| *Daily Mail* | *The People* |

Examples of broadsheet newspapers include:

| | |
|---|---|
| *The Times* | *The Observer* |
| *The Guardian* | *The Sunday Times* |
| *The Daily Telegraph* | *The Independent* |

#### Contrasting styles of tabloid and broadsheet newspapers

**The tabloid papers**

> A good, tight summary of features is often valuable in General Studies, especially in shorter written answers.

- are smaller in size, and thus easily folded, carried and read in crowded places like buses or trains
- have stories and articles that are brief and can be read quickly
- contain main stories that often focus on celebrities
- feature large photographic images on their front pages in order to catch the eye
- use puns in their headlines in order to attract attention
- follow a conventional pattern in their layout, so regular readers will know where to look for a particular feature
- are often very nationalistic, particularly in support of national sports teams (although virtually always the male sports, such as soccer, rugby, cricket and boxing)
- are usually cheaper than broadsheets.

**The broadsheet papers**

> Don't *assume* that examiners know the format of broadsheet newspapers, but make sure that you *do* know it!

- are of a larger size, making it more difficult to open and read them in confined spaces
- offer detailed analysis and description

- often have specialist reporters covering specific areas of news and current events
- use headlines designed to give an insight into the story or article that follows
- provide specialist supplements on a regular basis, covering topics designed to appeal to readers (such as education or information technology); these are often a vehicle for adverts for a range of managerial or other skilled employment.

## Political support by tabloids and broadsheets

*The Independent* and *The Independent on Sunday* follow no party line. They also do not print stories on the royal family, and will only mention them in terms of the specific involvement they might have had in relation to a particular news item.

Political influences of the Press should be understood. Make sure you know about the political views of newspapers.

With the exception of *The Independent* and the *Independent on Sunday*, all British newspapers support a political party, some more directly than others. *The Daily Telegraph*, *The Express* and *Daily Mail* have always been extremely pro-Conservative, while *The Guardian* has always taken a more radical line, and together with *The Mirror* has tended to support the Labour or Liberal Democrat parties. *The Sun* boasted that its support won the 1993 election for the Conservatives, although it changed sides in 1997 and urged its readers to vote for Tony Blair and Labour.

## Techniques used in newspapers

Newspapers influence their readers through a variety of techniques, most notably:

### Editorials

These are articles by the editor, setting out the views of the newspaper – often in a very partisan way.

### News stories

Particularly through the interpretation given to the stories, or their prominence within the contents.

### Cartoons

There is a long history of the political cartoon in the British Press.

### Articles

Sometimes written by prominent politicians.

### Letters

Which will usually support the political line taken by that newspaper and many of its readers.

### Photographs

It is said the camera never lies, but powerful images can be created to support the written word and give extremely powerful messages in support of the political angle being taken in a story.

> Sometimes newspapers, in addition to offering a general political viewpoint that readers absorb (perhaps unwittingly), will run direct political campaigns. For example, *The Sun* in 1999, despite its recent conversion to Labour and support of British membership of the European Union, ran a fierce campaign in favour of retaining the pound sterling, berating cabinet ministers, who it was thought, favoured monetary union.
>
> **KEY POINT**

## Arguments for and against limits on the freedom of the press

| | |
|---|---|
| AQA A | M1 |
| AQA B | M1, M2 |
| EDEXCEL | M1 |
| OCR | M1 |

The idea of censorship of the Press is not one that would find popular support in Great Britain, although in times of war the government is careful to control the flow of information given to the press. It does so with two primary justifications:

- it would be foolish to let the enemy know what was being planned

Do not assume there are no arguments for censorship in a democracy.

You need to be aware of these limits on the Press. You will not need to know the close detail of these restraints, but certainly an outline is important.

- the public can be shielded from potentially very damaging stories if things go wrong, and information revealed in a controlled way is less likely to lead to a collapse of morale – while, on the other hand, good news stories can be emphasised in order to increase national morale.

However, there are limitations on what the Press will print, some statutory (meaning 'established in law') and some voluntary.

### Statutory limitations

- The Official Secrets Act (the UK alone in the western democracies has such a law)
- The Obscene Publications Act
- The Contempt of Court Act.

### Voluntary limitations

- D-notices – requests from the Government not to print certain stories, often of a military nature
- Press Complaints Commission 'Code of Practice' – a voluntary code accepted by all newspapers, supposedly to guarantee rights for individuals against intrusion by journalists. (However, the code is often pushed to the limit by some newspapers, particularly when they are seeking stories about prominent people such as members of the royal family.)
- Sometimes editors accept a 'temporary news blackout' where reporting of a serious crime might hinder a police investigation, but this is only for the duration of the sensitive investigation time.

It is said by some that there should be firmer controls on the Press, particularly the Tabloids, because:

- they print damaging stories about famous people
- they treat people, especially women, in a demeaning way
- they reduce complex stories to a very simplistic level, often based on the individuals who are involved
- they are often jingoistic
- they create the idea that youth is the most important thing.

However, it must be remembered that the tabloids:

- are far more popular than the broadsheets in terms of sales
- argue that photographs of scantily clad women are 'fun' and not exploitative or demeaning
- claim to be meeting a need for 'light' news and popular entertainment
- argue that people are not forced to buy them – so if they do buy them, then the tabloids are clearly what people want.

### Progress check

1  What are the main differences between the tabloid and broadsheet newspapers?

2  Outline the main techniques used by the Press to influence their readers' political opinions.

2 Editorials; positioning and content of news stories; cartoons with a political message; articles supporting the political line of the paper, often written by politicians; letters from readers; photographic images.

Broadsheets: larger size, less convenient in a confined space; headlines lead into stories; analysis of events and items covered in articles; specialist reporters; usually more expensive.

very nationalistic; lacking in detailed analysis; usually cheaper.

1  Tabloids: smaller size; many stories based around personalities; eye-catching headlines and cover photos,

# 7.2 Television – 'the box in the corner'

**After studying this section you should be able to:**

- *compare and contrast the BBC with commercial TV companies, particularly in terms of funding*
- *identify characteristics of popular soap operas*
- *comment on the influence on society of violence in TV*

## The BBC versus the commercial companies

| AQA A | M1 |
|---|---|
| AQA B | M1 |
| EDEXCEL | M1 |
| OCR | M1 |

An early example of the power of TV.

The Pilkington Committee was a Royal Commission set up by the government to report on the future of broadcasting in Britain.

Reasons for expanding the number of channels.

Global broadcasting refers to the fact that television and radio can now be transmitted around the world through the use of satellites.

You should take a view on the power and development of satellite television around the world.

'South Park' (a cult cartoon made for a primarily adult audience) first appeared on Channel 4 and was then snapped up by a satellite channel in the late 1990s – a sign of the new order in TV.

A brief historical background of television is as follows:

- The BBC was first formed as an amalgamation of separate radio stations in 1922, gaining a Royal Charter and becoming the British Broadcasting *Corporation*, as opposed to *Company* (which it was first called) in 1926. TV trials were halted by the onset of World War II, so the first national television broadcasting came in 1946. The number of television set owners rocketed after the televising of the coronation of Queen Elizabeth II in 1953 – an event watched by millions of people (most people viewing it on other people's sets, i.e. several families congregated in one house to watch the TV set). This was the first time in almost a thousand years of such ceremonies that it had been witnessed by any more than a tiny social élite present in Westminster Abbey.

- Independent television first appeared in 1956 – its first advert being for toothpaste. However, the power of radio was still so strong that on the opening night of ITV (Independent television), BBC radio countered with a radio broadcast – Grace Archer, the matriarchal figure in the radio soap opera 'The Archers' was burned to death in a barn fire in that same evening's broadcast, which attracted a bigger audience than the opening of ITV.

- The Pilkington Committee recommended the setting up of BBC 2, which first broadcast in 1964, followed by Channel 4 in 1982. These stations were seen as a means of broadening TV, so that minority tastes and 'quality' programming could be catered for. This was not only in the realm of serious programmes – musical tastes were catered for in a series such as 'The Jazz Show' and the cult pop music show 'The Old Grey Whistle Test', while some comedy shows first broadcast on a trial basis on the 'minority' stations went on to achieve cult status, such as 'Monty Python's Flying Circus' (first broadcast in 1969). It was interesting that in Wales the fourth channel became a primarily Welsh language station in an attempt to strengthen and popularise the language throughout the Principality – producing not only entertainment, but also programmes for people who wished to learn Welsh.

- The fifty years since the televising of the first black-and-white programmes have seen a dramatic advance in broadcasting technology. 'Sky' television was launched in 1989 and the familiar satellite receivers have now become almost as common as the traditional aerials which pick up terrestrial (land-based) signals. The most recent developments have been in cable and satellite broadcasting. Important questions arise from the concentration of global broadcasting in the hands of a few media barons, such as Rupert Murdoch. Is the world getting a primarily Western view of events by watching global satellite television channels? Whatever your own personal view (and it is important that you consider this issue), it is important to be aware that today people have the option of choosing from a wide range of channels, including programmes from around the world. CNN news broadcasts have enabled global reporting, often supported by live pictures, to be beamed around the world. However, with so many different stations now available (and all except the BBC chasing the same companies to buy advertising time and the same

Do you think the expansion of available channels has led to a reduction in the quality of TV programming?

You need to be aware of the different funding mechanisms of the various TV channels.

This issue is one you should certainly have a view on and be able to discuss through actual examples.

audience to watch the adverts) the scramble for viewers has led many to talk about the 'dumbing down' of television, particularly independent television.

## The funding of the BBC

The BBC relies for its funding on the money it raises from the licence that every viewing household is required to purchase by law, by the sale of its programmes to foreign stations and through merchandising – for example, videos, cassettes and books. The licence fee is set by the government and it is illegal for the BBC to receive any income by advertising. On the other hand, independent channels, both terrestrial and satellite, gain most of their income from advertising. The advertising slots between the most popular programmes at the most popular times ('peak hours') attract the highest price – so it is in the commercial interest of ITV to attract mass audiences. Since it is the Government that sets the level of the licence fee and appoints the BBC's governing body, the BBC is forced to do its best to attract large popular audiences, especially for the peak hours between around 7.30 pm and 9.00 pm on weekdays. This has led to a 'ratings war', currently dominated by soap operas (a phrase originating with the sponsoring of popular programmes aimed primarily at housewives by US soap manufacturers in the 1950s). Many argue that this battle for viewers has been another contributing factor to the lowering of overall quality.

*Some key comparisons between the BBC and ITV*

| BBC | ITV |
|---|---|
| A national system, with local bases. | 14 regional franchises, each company supposed to reflect its local area. |
| Not based on profit, independent of business and commerce. | Income based on advertising revenue – franchise-holders able to use profits to subsidise other parts of their businesses. |
| Overall control of policy set by Governors, under their Chairman. | Controlled by Directors of the company. |
| Basic income from the licence fee – set by government. | Income to some extent set by the size of programme audiences – the more viewers, the higher the charge for adverts. |
| Economic freedom makes it easier to produce 'experimental' programmes that might not attract large audiences. | The need to generate as big an audience as possible for most programmes often leads to the use of tried and tested formulae in programme making. |

**KEY POINT**

## Soap operas

AQA A  M1
AQA B  M1
EDEXCEL  M1
OCR  M1

Think about the *nature* of the contents of the leading soap operas.

If you write about soaps in a General Studies exam, be objective in your analysis – no 'academic snobbery', nor subjective adulation!

The leading 'soaps' are *Coronation Street* on ITV and *EastEnders* on BBC – they present an interesting contrast of styles.

**Similarities**
- both are set in 'typical' working-class communities
- a lot of the action takes place in a pub, which acts as a place where groups of characters can be brought together
- both feature characters with strong regional accents
- an amazing number of dramatic incidents occur within a very small geographical area
- every episode ends with some incident that entices viewers to watch the next one.

**Differences**
- While the scripts of *Coronation Street* are often light and witty, those of *EastEnders* are more serious and sometimes violent.
- *EastEnders* tackles more social concerns, such as HIV/AIDS.

As the 'battle of the soaps' has hotted up, so the number of hours of broadcasts and the audiences have increased. Both the BBC and ITV know that they have captured huge audiences with these programmes.

## Violence on TV

| | |
|---|---|
| AQA A | M1 |
| AQA B | M1, M2 |
| EDEXCEL | M1 |
| OCR | M1 |

If you quote examples like this, remain objective and dispassionate, try to look at the facts not the emotion.

Examples of flawed studies – there is no conclusive evidence about the effects on behaviour of violence on TV.

Many people hold strong views about the links between TV and violent behaviour in society, but little has been proved. Notoriously, the young murderers of the child Jamie Bulger were alleged to have been watching a violent video with an 18 certificate before committing the murder. The notion of people living out their TV fantasies remains popular. Michael Ryan, the killer involved in the 'Hungerford Massacre' of 1988 was, according to the tabloid press, influenced by watching the Rambo films.

Some studies that allege to show a link between violence on TV and violence in society are flawed, e.g. Belson's 'Television and the Adolescent Boy' interviewed a group of boys who had *already* committed crimes, then asked them to comment on a list of programmes which were relatively violent when compared to most television programmes.

'The Portrayal of Violence in BBC Television' – a study carried out by Cumberbatch in 1989 – showed that British television was actually growing *less* violent in content than television in the USA. Research carried out in 1985 suggested that 40 per cent of children said they watched violent films on TV. However, when other researchers replicated the study in 1988, but added some non-existent titles, 68 per cent of the children claimed to have watched the non-existent films!

The jury is still out on this issue, but interesting questions can be posed for debate – although there are no clear answers to them:

In an exam, do not be afraid to say that you remain unsure, if that is a valid conclusion from the points you have raised.

- Does cartoon violence, such as that seen in a Tom and Jerry cartoon have any effect on children's behaviour?
- How is psychological violence measured for its effects?
- Are some people more prone to violence, with TV possibly providing a trigger?

> An Independent Broadcasting survey found 60 per cent of sample viewers thought that there was too much violence on television.
>
> Another IBA survey found that 6 per cent of viewers sometimes felt violent after watching violence on TV.
>
> A study in *New Society* (August 1987) reported that where people live causes violent behaviour as much as what they view on TV.

**KEY POINT**

## Progress check

1 Contrast the ways in which the BBC and the independent TV companies are financed.

2 What are some of the main features of soap operas?

3 Why can it be argued that there is no clear evidence as to the effects of TV violence on viewers?

3 Different studies have come to differing conclusions, and it is difficult to remove external factors, (such as housing, poverty, unemployment and crime) when trying to determine the extent to which TV viewing is to blame for an individual's behaviour.

2 They present a whole community as living in a very small area; lots of action and activities; nail-biting conclusions to episodes; supposedly representing ordinary people and their ordinary lives; extra excitement in stories when they are trying to boost audience figures (NB the Australian soaps, i.e. *Neighbours* and *Home and Away*, are more a series of tableau scenes featuring mainly glamorous young people in which the actual story line is largely coincidental).

1 BBC – licence fee, sale of programmes, sales of BBC products, such as videos, cassettes and books; ITV – sale of programmes, advertising.

# Sample question and model answer

**Step 1**
Introduction.

Your introduction should set out a framework – no more detail is required here.

**Step 2**
Development.

In the exam seek to identify and expand on separate points one at a time. Put the whole of one side of the argument first.

Then put the whole of the other side of the case.

Even if you feel strongly that one side is right, you should show that you know the whole range of arguments and be objective.

Come to a conclusion, where you can state your personal view.

Examine the view that attempts to impose greater limits on the Press constitute unwarranted interference.

- *'Greater' limits suggests that some limits already exist – try to name them.*
- *Be brief in the introduction – set out the basis of what you want to discuss in no more than two or three sentences.*
- **First**, *set out the arguments that further limits on the Press would be unwelcome, looking for examples to support your case. (These would be particularly good if they were very recent.) Most calls for further regulation/restriction are made concerning the tabloid press. Think about: examples of recent arguments over the freedom to write what are often very popular stories that sell lots of copies (some would say that the sales figures of papers like* The Sun *and* The News of the World *show how popular this style of journalism is).*
- *Instances where people in the public eye, such as politicians, clergy or teachers, have been exposed for some misdemeanour. Some people argue that to drag individuals down is unfair, but others would say that people who have been revealed as hypocrites deserve to be brought down by the Press.*
- *What right have people to argue that such popular writing should be limited – in a free society isn't the freedom to print a vital right?*
- *Would further regulation in effect amount to censorship, and set a dangerous precedent – one that is based at best on snobbery, and at worst is politically sinister?*
- *The argument that popular stories in the tabloids are often just seen as fun – if individuals feel wronged they can always sue the newspaper.*
- *The fact that the royal family are often the focus of media stories – on the one hand they need publicity, but on the other, does this sometimes go too far?*

*But*

- *The tabloid press is often vulgar, male-biased and intrusive.*
- *Whether it is always true that people should be free to read what they want to.*
- *Lives can be damaged and reputations ruined for no valid reason by the Press:*
  - *We all have a right to enjoy freedom as individuals in a free society – including those people who find themselves being hounded*
  - *the tabloid press demeans those it exploits for profit, and those who buy such papers*
  - *the voluntary Code of Conduct of the Press Complaints Commission is simply ignored when the tabloids choose to do so – a legally binding Code is needed in order to control them.*
- *Using the arguments you have set out, without repeating in detail, summarise the case and, if it is appropriate (and it very often is in General Studies), state your personal views, for example:*

*It is clear that on occasion the Press goes too far, but it is also clear that an apology is quickly made if it is clear that public opinion is upset. Public opinion acts as a 'moral censor', and this should represent the limits of control, together with the industry's own Code of Conduct. To go further, to introduce government controls would be a step too far – a step towards the possible end of the vital democratic cornerstone of the freedom of the Press.*

## Practice examination questions

### Short answer questions

1 What are the main defining features of the tabloid press?

2 In what circumstances might a degree of censorship be justified in the British press?

3 Why are soap operas not really a reflection of society?

### Essay question

4 Discuss the issues that arise from the freedom of the popular press to publish stories about the private lives of famous people who are in the public eye.

# Chapter 8
# *The nature of science*

*The following topics are covered in this chapter:*

- The different types of science
- Key developments in the history of science

## 8.1 The different types of science

**After studying this section you should be able to:**

- list the different types of science that exist and give examples of some of their subject divisions
- outline some basic methods and principles involved in science
- identify the difference between deductive and inductive thinking

*LEARNING SUMMARY*

### Characteristics of the sciences

| AQA A | M2 |
| AQA B | M1, M2, M3 |
| EDEXCEL | M2 |
| OCR | M2 |

The sciences can be divided into three main areas: physical sciences, life (or biological) sciences, earth sciences.

Each of these areas is then subdivided into different specific subjects:

| **Physical sciences** | *which subdivide into things like:* |
| Physics | mechanics |
| Chemistry | physical and bio-chemistry |
| Astronomy | cosmology (study of the universe). |

| **Life sciences** | *which subdivide into:* |
| Biology | physiology, anatomy |
| Botany | mycology (study of fungi) |
| Zoology | ornithology (study of birds). |

| **Earth sciences** | *which includes:* |
| Geology | palaeontology, seismology, geophysics, geochemistry, palaeobiology. |

However, it should always be remembered that the simplistic classification given above masks the fact that science often has inter-locking relationships between elements that appear in separate areas. For example, the identification of DNA (deoxyribonucleic acid) came about following work containing elements of biology (a life science) and chemistry (a physical science).

**Applied sciences**

These are areas where scientific knowledge and understanding is applied in ways that are of direct practical use to people. These include:

- metallurgy, electronics, aeronautics *(applied physical sciences)*
- medicine, agronomy *(applied life sciences)*.

'Science' comes from the Latin word *Scientia* – 'to know'. It denotes a systematised knowledge arising from the organisation of objectively verifiable evidence. The academic pursuit of systematised knowledge arising from the organisation of objectively verifiable evidence is known as 'pure' science; the pursuit of science in order to use its discoveries in a practical way is known as 'applied' science.

*KEY POINT*

## Scientific methods

A model, or 'paradigm' is an attempt to produce a pattern or reproduction (especially one supporting a theory) to explain why observable phenomena occur. These can sometimes enable us to make predictions of what will occur in the future, or in other situations.

Physical processes: to do with material objects in the universe.

Applied mathematics is that branch of mathematics that seeks to put the study to practical use in such diverse fields as mechanics and astronomy.

The use of mathematics in constructing physical theories makes them precise and comprehensive.

### Models

Possibly the only thing that all areas of scientific study have in common is that they seek to provide conclusions based on firm evidence.

The **physical sciences** seek to produce models (paradigms) which are comprehensive. Such models are then used to explain physical processes that vary in scale from the sub-atomic ($10^{-15}$m, or less) to the astronomical (billions of kilometres), and these vary in time from about $10^{-24}$ seconds through to billions of years. Such models can also allow for accurate predictions to be made – a good example of their use would be the way in which NASA scientists were able to launch space craft that reached their destination with great accuracy, even when it was the first time such a journey had been made.

Galileo (1564–1642) and Descartes (1596–1650) were the first to insist that science should use only precise mathematical concepts in its theories. (Previously, theory had been founded in plausible possibility based on observation, and increasingly during the Middle Ages on whether it was supported by Biblical writing.) The application of such theory to physical reality involves making a calculation using applied mathematics. It is this that makes physical theories so comprehensive and such precise predictors.

However, not all scientific study can reach such a level of mathematical certainty.

> **KEY POINT**
>
> Scientific study seeks mathematical support for comprehensiveness and precision, but if this is not possible it does not mean that conclusions reached in other ways have to be rejected. Look, for example, at Darwin's Theory of Evolution or Pasteur's belief that it was germs that spread disease – neither of these had a mathematical basis.

It would be wrong to think that all models always agree with each other – and this presents a dilemma for scientists. For example, two current theories widely accepted in Physics are those relating to quantum mechanics (which seeks to explain atomic processes), and these and the General Theory of Relativity (which explains astronomical processes) are mutually inconsistent. Physicists can accept both of these theories, accept the inconsistencies and recognise that this is an area still requiring resolution. It would thus be wrong to say that scientists think they have found all the answers – they often admit to still having questions to which they seek answers.

### Experimentation

Experimentation is central to scientific methodology. It is used to verify in an observable way 'hypotheses' that have been developed. A hypothesis is a suggested explanation for a collection of known facts. If an experiment is successful a hypothesis may be elevated to the more certain status of **theory**.

> **KEY POINT**
>
> Scientists often seek to build theories supported by specially designed experiments. Such experiments are often used to test a *hypothesis*.

## Two types of scientific thinking

Scientists use two types of thinking when trying to prove or disprove a hypothesis: **deductive thinking** and **inductive thinking**.

Inductive thinking is the more usual, since the essence of much science and scientific thought is that it is philosophically difficult to be certain that something which is observable and demonstrable *now* will always remain in the same state in the future and in all states.

## Deductive thinking

This involves a line of thought containing a series of premises that are all true. It is therefore impossible for a conclusion arrived at from these to be false, since the information contained in the conclusion is already found in the premises, e.g.:

All humans are mammals.
All mammals have livers.
We therefore deduce that all humans have livers.

Think about experiments you have done in school science lessons – they *assume* a common outcome will happen every time the experiment is carried out.

## Inductive thinking

This thinking has a conclusion that goes *beyond* the information contained in the premise – so it is *assuming* that if the same thing can be observed over and over again with the same outcome, then the outcome *has* to be the same, e.g.:

All observed polar bears are white.
Therefore *all* polar bears, whether they have been seen or not, are white.

However, this type of thinking, which occurs a lot in science, is not certain and can let us down, e.g.:

All observed swans are white.
Therefore *all* swans are white.

**Deduce** = infer by reasoning from given facts.

**Induce** = infer by reasoning from particular cases to general conclusions.

This might have been thought to have been true until the discovery of Australia, where it was observed that swans are black!

## Two important scientific terms

| | |
|---|---|
| AQA A | M2 |
| AQA B | M1, M2, M3 |
| EDEXCEL | M2 |
| OCR | M2 |

In 1758 The Swedish biologist Carolus Linnaeus published his classification of all known species using two names – the first being the genus (family) and the second an adjective which is often descriptive e.g. *Homo* (man) *sapiens* (wise).

There are two terms which are used quite frequently in science:

**Laws**
- a generalised, or universal formulation based on a series of events or processes observed to recur regularly under certain conditions;
- or universal patterns in nature/universal generalisations.

**Classification**
- scientists seek to provide a sense of order, and classification helps provide a means of logical arrangement. Plants and animals are classified into families while chemists have the Periodic Table which classifies all known elements into groups to show the relationship between them.

## Progress check

1 Name the three main branches of the physical sciences.

2 Physiology and anatomy are examples of what branch of the sciences?

3 Name two applied physical sciences.

4 What is the name given to models that are put forward to explain physical processes?

5 Name the French mathematician and philosopher who believed that as far as possible science should be based on mathematical concepts.

6 What is the characteristic of inductive thinking?

7 What is the name given to a generalised, or universal formulation that is based on a series of events or processes which can be observed to recur regularly under certain conditions?

8 For what is the scientist Linnaeus best remembered?

1 Physical, Life and Earth.
2 Biology.
3 Two from metallurgy, electronics or aeronautics.
4 Paradigms.
5 Descartes.
6 It has a conclusion that goes beyond the information contained in the premise.
7 A law.
8 His classification of all known species, published in 1758.

# 8.2 Some key developments in the history of science

**After studying this section you should be able to:**

- list important discoveries relating to matter
- describe landmarks in discoveries about energy
- cite discoveries relating to the natural world and living things

## Discoveries about matter

| AQA A | M2 |
|---|---|
| AQA B | M1, M2, M3 |
| EDEXCEL | M2 |
| OCR | M2 |

**Matter** can be defined as 'that of which all physical objects consist' (*Penguin English Dictionary*). It belongs to the Physical Sciences.

**1661** Robert Boyle suggests that small moving particles can explain chemical reactions.

**1666** Isaac Newton describes how minute particles can attract and repel each other; also invents calculus and starts to work on gravity.

**18th c.** Researchers study heat and investigate newly discovered gases.

**1789** Lavoisier, the father of modern chemistry, publishes *Treatise on Chemical Elements* which is the start of quantitative chemistry – it was he who first correctly identified oxygen.

**1808** Dalton introduces the modern chemical ideas of elements and compounds made from atoms and molecules.

**1830** German chemists start to focus on the realisation that carbon lies at the heart of organic and biochemistry; they isolate carbon as being fundamental to all life.

**1869** Mendeleyev devises the Periodic Table, classifying elements into similar groups by their atomic weight.

**1897** Thomson discovers electrons, suggesting that atoms are not (after all) the smallest particles.

**1900** Important new chemical industries develop, including the manufacture of synthetic drugs and dyes.

**20th c.** Developments have included:
- harnessing x-rays for medical use
- mass production of radios, telephones, etc. from bakelite – a synthetic plastic, which creates a trade and development in plastics (which then grows into one of the world's major industries)
- on exploration of the central nucleus of an atom, even smaller particles are found – first protons and neutrons, later even smaller sub-atomic particles called quarks are discovered
- the World War II period (1939–45) gives a huge stimulus to work on the atomic bomb and on medical advances such as antibiotics and plastic surgery
- the post-war development of synthetic fibres such as nylon for making cheaper clothes.

## Discoveries about energy

| AQA A | M2 |
|---|---|
| AQA B | M1, M2, M3 |
| EDEXCEL | M2 |
| OCR | M2 |

**16th c.** Galileo insists on using experiment and mathematics in his studies in exploring nature, rather than on plausible possibilities based on observation (which had previously been thought to be sufficient).

**1687** Newton publishes his Theory of Gravity, a single mathematical law describing the movement of distant planets, as well as objects on Earth.

# The nature of science

Energy is a power or force, or the capability for doing work. It is usually associated with physics, one of the physical sciences.

| | |
|---|---|
| 18th c. | Arguments occur between those supporting Newton's view that light consists of tiny particles and those supporting Huygen's (a Dutch physicist) view that light is made from waves. |
| 1745 | The Leyden Jar invented, which could store static electricity so that electrical experiments could be carried out. |
| 1760s | First commercial use of steam engines for pumping water out of mines – later developed into locomotives. |
| 1799 | The Italian physicist Volta invented the battery – the first source of current electricity (i.e. electricity that can be controlled rather than existing solely in lightning). |
| 19th c. | Using mathematical techniques and experiments, the wave theory of light is established.

Faraday uses magnetic forces as a basis for making a dynamo – crucial in supplying electricity.

Physicists such as Joule undertake work on the relationship between heat, power and work.

Machines become ever more important.

'The Railway Age' arrives. |
| 1888 | Hertz creates radio waves – a vital discovery for modern science and technology. |
| Late 19th c. | Public gas and electricity networks transform domestic and industrial life.

The phonograph and moving films are invented – marking the birth of the entertainment industry. |
| 1915 | Einstein revolutionises the view of the universe by his General Theory of Relativity. |
| 20th c. | Development of quantum mechanics, suggesting that light is a stream of tiny protons that act as waves and particles.

More is learned about radio-activity as the internal structure of the atomic nucleus is investigated. |
| 1945 | Completion of the first atomic bomb. |
| Late 20th c. | Nuclear energy harnessed for electricity generation.

Travelling speeds increase, e.g. Concorde and high-speed trains.

Space travel developed during 1960s, culminating in a human landing on the moon in 1969. |
| 1979 | Physicists link electromagnetic and weak nuclear forces, thus developing understanding of nuclei and the composition of atoms. |

## Discoveries about the natural world

| AQA A | M2 |
|---|---|
| AQA B | M1, M2, M3 |
| EDEXCEL | M2 |
| OCR | M2 |

The natural world refers to that which occurs in nature without having to be artificially prepared. It can cover all the fields of science, but is primarily associated with the life and earth sciences.

| | |
|---|---|
| 1543 | Copernicus (a Pole) suggests that the behaviour of heavenly bodies is better explained by the Earth moving round the sun. |
| 1608 | Invention of the telescope. |
| 1609 | Kepler (a German) publishes his first two laws of planetary motion. |
| 1610 | Galileo (an Italian) makes his first observation of the stars by telescope. |
| 1611 | de Dominis (an Italian) publishes a scientific explanation for the rainbow. |
| 1644 | Torricelli (an Italian) invents the barometer – used to forecast weather from 1660. |
| 1666 | Newton measures the moon's orbit. His view of a sun-centred planetary system held together by gravity gains popularity. |

| 1705 | Halley (English) predicts the return of a comet in 1758 (eventually named after him). |
|---|---|
| 18th c. | New and more accurate instruments enable people to record and collect data about the atmosphere – the new science of meteorology. |
| | Explorers like James Cook undertake long scientific journeys – maps improve and information is gathered on plants, animals and societies. |
| 1781 | Herschel (a British astronomer) maps the stars and discovers Uranus. |
| 1830 | Lyell (a British geologist) suggests that the Earth has been slowly changing over a long period. |
| 1868 | Helium (one of the lightest elements) is first seen in the spectrum of the sun. |
| 1896 | Becquerel (a Frenchman) discovers radio-activity, which can measure the age of fossils. |
| 1908 | An enormous new telescope is built at Mount Wilson observatory in California. |
| 1915 | Wegener (a German) published the evidence for continental drift (not widely accepted until 1960). |
| 1935 | Pluto discovered as knowledge of the universe continues to grow. Radio-telescopes enable the distant universe to be surveyed – theories about the origins of the universe, and creation itself become the centre of scientific debate. |
| 1935 | Richter (an American) devises the scale for measuring the size of earthquakes. |
| 1959 | The first artificial object leaves the Earth's atmosphere and goes into orbit – Sputnik I. |
| 1960s | The 'Space Race' is a political as well as scientific challenge to the Soviet Union and the United States. |
| 1969 | Neil Armstrong takes the first human steps on the moon. |
| 1970s | Weather forecasting becomes far more accurate with the aid of satellites and computers. |
| | Complex theories about the creation of the universe are put forward. The work of scientists like Stephen Hawking on Black holes has been very important. |
| 1997 | Scientists at Sussex University analysing information gained from the Hubble Telescope estimate that the universe is at least 13 billion years old. |

## Discoveries about living things

| AQA A | M2 |
|---|---|
| AQA B | M1, M2, M3 |
| EDEXCEL | M2 |
| OCR | M2 |

**Living things** covers the study of things from the microscopic to the largest living creature on Earth – the blue whale. It can include studies in evolution based on the study of variations in contemporary plants and animals. It belongs to the life sciences.

| 16th c. | Start of dissection of human bodies to find out how the human anatomy works are led by Vesalius (an Italian). |
|---|---|
| 1626 | Santorio (an Italian) measures the temperature of the human body. |
| 1628 | Harvey describes the circulation of blood and the role of the heart. |
| 1749 | Linnaeus (a Swede) publishes his classification of plants and animals using two Latin names. |
| 18th c. | The first suggestions are made that living things had been slowly changing since the Earth was created (e.g. the work of French naturalist Georges-Louis Buffon). |
| 19th c. | The discovery of new fossils leads to the view that species can become extinct. |
| | Lamarck puts forward the theory that animals pass on environmental adaptations to offspring. |

| | |
|---|---|
| | German researchers show that cells are the basic unit of both plant and animal life. |
| 1859 | Darwin publishes *On the Origin of Species* to support his Theory of Evolution. |
| 1860s | Pasteur shows that fermentation is due to micro-organisms, and invents a way of killing harmful microbes in wine and beer. |
| 20th c. | Modern genetic theories are developed after earlier work by Gregor Mendel on heredity in peas. |
| | Biochemists identify the importance of chemicals such as vitamins and hormones. |
| | The development of antibiotics in the second half of the century transforms healthcare. |
| | The new science of molecular biology leads to studies of the nature of genes and reproduction. |
| 1953 | Watson and Crick discover DNA – the chemical responsible for heredity – and this revolutionises biology. |
| 1980s | The discovery is made that acid rain caused by pollution in one country can destroy vast areas of natural vegetation in other countries. |
| 1990s | Controversial new techniques in genetic engineering enable work in: 'disease free' animals; genetically modified food; cloning. |

## Progress check

1 What contribution did Mendeleyev make to modern chemistry?

2 Who were the first to claim that science should seek to base itself on experiments and mathematical models?

3 What is measured on the Richter Scale, first formulated in 1935?

4 What name was given to the first space vehicle to leave the Earth's atmosphere and go into orbit, launched in 1959?

5 What was the title of Charles Darwin's book on evolution, first published in 1859?

6 What was discovered by Watson and Crick in 1953 that revolutionised biology?

7 Name three new areas of work that are currently being pursued in the field of genetic engineering.

7 Disease-free animals, genetically modified food and cloning.
6 DNA (deoxyribonucleic acid).
5 *On the Origin of Species.*
4 Sputnik I.
3 Earthquakes.
2 Galileo and Descartes.
1 He devised the Periodic Table, classifying elements into similar groups by their atomic weight.

## Sample question and model answer

To what extent can it be argued that since science uses mainly inductive methods its results can never be proved to be correct?

**Step 1**
Introduction: Define what is meant by 'inductive'.

*Induction = a way of reasoning from particular cases to general conclusions, e.g. because an experiment has come out in the same way for a hundred consecutive times, it will always come out in that way.*

**Step 2**
Show how science uses inductive methods – then show why this does not *prove* correctness.

- *Inductive methods are at the heart of experimentation – but this only shows the result of that particular experiment on that occasion and cannot make any future predictions that the same result will **always** happen when the experiment is repeated in the future.*

- *Some examples (such as the ones provided in this chapter) might be given to further illustrate the nature of inductive reasoning.*

- *Inductive reasoning proceeds from specific observations and/or experiments to more general hypothesis and reason.*

- *Certainty can not be achieved by induction alone.*

- *Inductive reasoning can be contrasted with deductive reasoning – where it can be claimed that a conclusion is true because every premise that precedes that conclusion is true.*

- *For the scientist, induction is an important idea and the work of a scientist needs to be based as far as possible on objectivity and observation, with no preconceptions of what an outcome is likely to be and the need to avoid falsification.*

- *A mathematical model that supports a particular theory gives it precision and reinforces it – particularly in the physical sciences, which is why mathematics is so important in the study of physics.*

**Step 3**
Conclusion.

*Having shown the examiner that you understand what is meant by induction, and provided as many examples as you can to illustrate this, you should conclude that inductive methods, while suggesting that something is correct, cannot in themselves offer final, definite proof that this is the case.*

*For example:*

It has been said that since all observed ravens are black, then it holds that all ravens are black. However, there may be, somewhere in the world, a white raven that nobody has yet observed. We cannot prove or disprove the existence of such a bird, but if it does exist the claim that all ravens are black is immediately invalidated. Similarly, it might once have been claimed that all swans were white and so far as all Europeans up to the time of the voyages by Captain Cook this was the observable 'reality'. However, on arrival in Australia it became obvious that swans in that country were black and the theory that had previously been apparently observably correct suddenly became incorrect. Inductive methodology plays an important role in the sciences and in experimentation but the title is correct in its assertion that its results can never be finally proved to be correct.

## Practice examination questions

### Short answer questions

**1** What is meant by 'inductive methodology'?

**2** What is the difference between a hypothesis and a law?

**3** Why do many scientists place an emphasis on classification?

### Essay question

**4** Why did Darwin's *The Origin of Species* create such a huge and, to a few, an abiding controversy?

# Chapter 9
# Morality and science

**The following topics are covered in this chapter:**

- *Science and technology – good, bad and ugly*
- *Ethical dilemmas in science and technology*
- *Environmental concerns*

## 9.1 Science and technology – good, bad and ugly

**After studying this section you should be able to:**

- *outline ways in which science and technology have changed our life-style*
- *describe the gulf that exists between the lifestyles of those who live in the economically developed world and those in the under-developed world*
- *argue the case for and against the arms trade*

LEARNING SUMMARY

### Our changing lifestyle

| | |
|---|---|
| AQA A | M2 |
| AQA B | M1, M2, M3 |
| EDEXCEL | M2 |
| OCR | M2 |

One of the purposes of General Studies as a subject is to consider issues that are of lasting importance to the world – and such issues over the last century have increasingly been dominated by science and technology. It has been said that more things have been invented and discovered in the past 50 years than in the rest of history added together. During this time humanity has, for example, developed the ability both to cure many more sick people, while also discovering the means to obliterate the whole of humanity through nuclear weaponry. Science and technology raise some really crucial questions that affect the very basis of our contemporary lifestyle. In a General Studies examination you might well be asked to discuss issues such as:

- the gap between the advanced and the developing economies of the world, and the abilities of developing countries to make use of scientific and technological developments
- whether scientists are trying to 'play God' by 'interfering' with nature (for example, in areas such as genetic engineering)
- whether the rich world will bring about its own destruction through creating global warming
- the rich world creating situations that have the effect of making the gap between them and the poorest countries ever wider.

Despite these various serious considerations, many would claim that advances in science and technology mean that:

- we are now better fed, housed and educated than at any other time in history and the resources that have enabled us to reach this state have in large part come about because of technological advances
- medical advances mean that diseases that once killed many people (such as measles) are now routinely dealt with
- we are the first people in history who regard global communications and travel as routine – the idea of package holidays to Africa would have seemed bizarre until very recently, but the technology of jet aircraft makes it increasingly commonplace today

107

- satellite technology opens up huge opportunities, e.g.:
  - 'distance learning' for remote communities
  - the monitoring of pollution and the damage to the ozone layer
  - the ability to understand global weather patterns more fully, so that people in vulnerable areas can be better protected
  - global communications: TV, radio, telephone.

One thing that is clear is that people living in the countries that have advanced economies are on the whole enjoying a standard of living that has never been rivalled. Over the last century we have moved from a situation where electricity was just beginning to be introduced into family homes to a situation where many homes now have a:

> You should be able to discuss how such things have changed people's lives and leisure patterns.

- television
- radio
- video recorder
- computer
- hi-fi system.

Consider also that a century ago most long-distance journeys were made by steam train and local journeys by bus or tram. Today most journeys, even very short local journeys, are made by car. However, greater use of the car has brought major problems to society:

- people living in small, rural communities have often lost all their public transport and those without a car can be very isolated
- the growth of individual car journeys is one of the major causes of pollution and is being linked increasingly to the rise in diseases such as asthma.

## Problems for the less economically developed countries

| | |
|---|---|
| AQA A | M2 |
| AQA B | M1, M2, M3 |
| EDEXCEL | M2 |
| OCR | M2 |

Looked at globally, people's life-styles vary widely. For many millions of people who live in the less economically developed world the gap between the quality of their lives and those living in the West does not get any smaller:

- many homes contain no water, electricity or sanitation
- many children never grow to see adulthood
- many simple medical operations are not carried out because the resources – doctors, medicines, hospitals – do not exist
- the idea of ever owning items such as cars or hi-fi systems, is beyond the dreams of many – and in any case there are few roads on which one could run a car and no electricity to power a hi-fi in many rural areas in the less economically developed world.

> **KEY POINT**
> The benefits brought by science and technology have not been evenly spread. The 'rich' world has seen its way of life transformed over the last 100 years, but this is simply not the case for millions in the 'poor' world.

> Questions such as these may well form the basis of exam questions.

If we accept that the advances brought about by science and technology have not been evenly shared among the peoples of the world should we be concerned about this? Should someone who has a scientific training – who seeks to be objective, to base work on observation and experiment in a very specific area – be expected to consider the wider social, or ethical, aspects of their work? Albert Einstein, whose work proved so important in the developments that led to the creation of the atomic bombs dropped on Hiroshima and Nagasaki, was quoted as having said that if he had realised what he was doing he would have become a clock maker instead.

## The arms industry – a trade in death, or a hope for future world stability?

One of the biggest areas of trade that exists with less economically developed countries is that in arms. The United Kingdom is one of the world's biggest manufacturers and sellers of military equipment, together with other countries such as the United States, France, Italy and Russia. This is an issue that you might well be asked to consider in a General Studies exam – world conflicts have been a feature of history, but what are the pros and cons of the arms trade and is it ethical for the British government to sell arms to other countries?

The arguments for and against arms trading can be summarised as follows.

| *For the arms trade* | *Against the arms trade* |
| --- | --- |
| Independent nations all have the right to oppose aggression – and should therefore have the means to do so. | By selling weapons, Britain is encouraging some of the poorest countries on Earth to use too great a share of their limited resources on military matters, rather than on social and economic development. |
| Britain can exercise some moral authority through negotiating deals with the government to which it sells weapons. | Many such countries cannot afford to spend so much on weapons – and so they remain in debt to Britain and the other arms trading countries, which is morally unacceptable. |
| There are many examples, even in the poorest countries, of opposition groups (both internal and external) trying to bring down the legitimate government. Political stability is encouraged by enabling a government to defend itself. | Arming other nations makes the concept of world peace even more difficult to achieve. |
| Weapons themselves are not a cause, but are simply a symptom of the causes of war. UK intelligence services know which countries want guns for offensive purposes and the government agrees that there *is* an ethical element in its arms sales policy. | Military capability encourages aggressive nationalism in even the smallest and economically weakest country. |
| It is not easy to limit conventional weapons and national armies – what right has Britain got to try to influence the internal policies of countries that want to spend their own money on weapons – isn't that an internal matter for the people of the country? | The arms trade is a major way in which the richest countries exercise influence and control over the poorest in a post-colonial world. This is immoral and as a country we should seek to set a moral standard by encouraging the poorest countries to develop into modern states, able to join the world's trading nations on a more equitable foundation. |
| There is no effective example in history of a country disarming itself and surviving to tell the story – 'disarmament' is a fine theory, but cannot happen in practice. | By assisting countries in maintaining armies we encourage a military élite who are naturally prone to warlike ambition, both internally and externally, in their country. |
| If Britain withdrew from the arms trade other countries would simply expand their trade and take over – and Britain would lose influence in the world. | Ending the arms trade would give Britain a strong moral position that would strengthen its arguments for world peace – to talk of this while selling guns around the world is inconsistent. |
| In many countries professional soldiers are intended to uphold peace – they need the capability to do this. | Britain would do better to help provide resources that encourage the development of industry, trade and prosperity around the world, instead of taking money for providing weapons of destruction. |
| In the UK, hundreds of thousands of people rely, either directly or indirectly, on the arms industry for their livelihoods. If this was severely curtailed the repercussions for some British communities would be devastating – we should develop alternatives before we run down the arms industry, or the UK government would be failing many of its citizens. | The skills of those who currently work in the UK arms industry could be transferred to the manufacture of socially useful products for the world as a whole – this could help to bring about a better global development, co-operation and peace. |

> **KEY POINT**
> The sale of military technology and weapons to less economically developed countries often accounts for a disproportionately high level of the spending of the governments of such countries – but you cannot simply say the trade should therefore immediately cease; you must consider arguments for the international arms trade carefully.

## Progress check

1 How has satellite technology supported the spread of education, particularly in countries lacking a well-developed system of education?

2 Why are routine medical operations often not performed in less economically developed countries?

3 Why might a reduction in Britain's arms sales to other countries lead to economic difficulties for some UK communities?

4 Apart from the UK, name two other European countries with a large arms trade.

5 Name five examples of electrical equipment that have helped to transform domestic entertainment.

5 Television, radio, video recorders, computers, hi-fi.
4 France and Italy.
3 Some towns have their economic base in factories that produce arms and military equipment – a reduction in the arms trade would cause unemployment.
2 The medical technology is known, but the economic resources to buy it and to pay medical staff is often lacking.
1 Through distance learning (with teaching packages) being beamed from satellites.

# 9.2 Ethical dilemmas in science and technology

**After studying this section you should be able to:**

- identify several ethical dilemmas relative to medical advances
- describe some major issues of concern relating to industrial and technological developments

> In a General Studies exam you should seek to present balanced arguments – although often you can also express a personal conclusion.

The world trade in arms is only one ethical debate on which a candidate for a General Studies exam should be able to take a balanced view. You should demonstrate the ability to weigh up all the arguments and, where appropriate, come to a personal conclusion as to which are the most compelling.

## Medical issues

| | |
|---|---|
| AQA A | M2 |
| AQA B | M1 |
| EDEXCEL | M2 |
| OCR | M2 |

> These points each highlight key debates. There is no easy right or wrong answer – you will need to develop your own perspective. Read around the issues, watch informed documentaries and listen to experts putting their differing points of view.

> Although public opinion cannot directly influence product development in medical research companies, such companies often have shareholders and will be in competition for government (or health department) finding, so there can be an indirect influence.

Several major ethical debates hinge on areas of medical advance, such as:

- Should doctors always be obliged to strive to keep people alive at all costs? (Should, for example, people who are terminally ill be allowed to ask a doctor to terminate their lives before its natural conclusion?)

- Should women be allowed to freeze their eggs so they can delay having children until they have achieved their career goals?

- Should scarce medical resources be concentrated on very expensive treatment that will keep some people alive, or should they be used to treat a greater number of people with non life-threatening illnesses, but whose lives might be quite severely affected without treatment?

- Should medical research companies concentrate their work on developing expensive new treatments largely for the benefit of people living in the rich world (such as Viagra), or should they concentrate on mass-producing cures for the basic illnesses that still kill millions of people in the less economically developed world?

## Industrial and technological issues

AQA A    M2
AQA B    M1, M2, M3
EDEXCEL    M2
OCR    M2

Other debates concern industrial and technological developments and relate to the dangers of pollution and environmental damage. We will look at these in more detail later on but, in brief, these issues include the following:

### The cost to the natural environment over the last century

There has always been localised pollution around urban centres, but this has become international (for example, British pollution affecting Scandinavian lakes and forests in the form of acid rain).

### Global warming

Changes to world weather patterns and rising sea levels threaten the world in a variety of ways, and particularly those millions of people who live in low-lying areas, often with little immediate chance of moving elsewhere (for example, much of the population of Bangladesh).

### Scarce resources

Is it feasible to expect that the developed economies of the world will ever reduce their consumption of the world's resources?

Although agreeing that too much pollution exists, too much damage is being done to our world and that we are exploiting the world for our own benefit, how many of us would agree to a reduced standard of living and quality of lifestyle? Just think of how much electricity we use in pursuit of our current lifestyle – for example, in work, for cooking our food, for recreational purposes (remember your battery-powered Walkman has used a lot of electricity in its manufacture), in travel by electric trains, or in the manufacture of our cars and so on – and then consider the fact that generating this electricity is a major cause of pollution around the world (whether it is generated using fossil fuels or by nuclear generation).

> Consider the arguments in favour of sustainable energy sources – wind and water for example. Is this a hope for the future?

### The increasing population of many countries

Not all pollution is caused by economically advanced countries. In some under-developed countries there are examples of deforestation – either for fuel or because the land is being cleared so that new areas of farming and food production can be opened up. This process is extremely damaging not only to the local environment but also to the wider world:

- on several recent occasions much of Indonesia has been affected by smog caused by the clearing and burning of forest trees

- the destruction of the tropical rainforest in recent years has been cited as a major reason for changes in the balance of the atmosphere (since carbon dioxide is no longer absorbed by the trees in such large quantities, it is forming a larger proportion of the atmosphere).

Increasing world population also relates to the ethical problem of artificial birth control. In countries where the Roman Catholic faith is strong many believe that contraception is morally wrong. (This is an issue we shall return to in the next chapter, when we look at some of the clashes that arise between science and technology, and culture and ideology.)

> There are huge dilemmas being posed by medical, scientific and industrial development. Most people in the UK now have a higher standard of living than ever before – but there is much talk of the Earth being at risk. How can we strike a balance, and how should scientists and technologists view ethical concerns in undertaking their work?
>
> **KEY POINT**

## Progress check

1  What medical dilemma hinges on the question of balance in the use of resources?

2  How has pollution created in Britain affected countries in Scandinavia?

3  What process that is affecting the whole world will have serious consequences for low-lying countries like Bangladesh?

4  Which country has been badly affected by smog caused by the burning of large areas of forest?

5  What aspect of Roman Catholic teaching poses a dilemma for many countries that have rapidly rising populations?

5 The doctrine that artificial contraception is wrong.
4 Indonesia.
3 Global warming will lead to a rise in sea level as the polar ice caps reduce.
2 Acid rain formed as a result of pollution in Britain falls onto Scandinavia – its effects are most notable in lakes and forests.
1 Whether to provide expensive treatment to keep a few people alive, or use the same money to provide more routine treatment for many more people to give them a much enhanced quality of life.

# 9.3 Environmental concerns

## After studying this section you should be able to:

- specify problems arising from air pollution
- describe the effects of water pollution
- outline arguments for and against genetically modified food
- present arguments for and against the use of nuclear power for electricity generation

## Air pollution

| AQA A | M2 |
| AQA B | M3 |
| EDEXCEL | M2 |
| OCR | M2 |

In today's world, industrial countries generate *millions* of tons of pollutants every year, many of which come from identifiable sources. Some examples of these pollutants and their effects are given in Table 9.1.

| Cause | Effect |
| --- | --- |
| Emission of sulphur dioxide from factories and power stations by burning coal or oil | Poisonous gases released into the atmosphere – the gas can destroy vegetation |
| | Dissolves in rainwater to form sulphuric acid – attacks marble and limestone (including buildings, statues, etc.) |
| Emission of hydrocarbons from vehicle exhausts and industry | Creation of ozone through interaction with sunlight – serious consequences for people with breathing difficulties when ozone levels increase |
| Emission of carbon monoxide and nitrogen oxides by internal combustion engines and industry | Carbon monoxide is one of the deadliest gases in the atmosphere – hence its use in many suicide attempts when exhaust fumes are breathed in |

*Table 9.1 Air pollutants and their effects*

### The greenhouse effect

This phrase describes a situation in which solar energy enters the atmosphere, but the re-emission of infra-red radiation from Earth is reduced. The 'greenhouse gas' carbon dioxide is particularly significant in this effect because it allows the sun's rays to penetrate the atmosphere, but not all the heat can then escape to balance this – with the result that the Earth is slowly warming up like a greenhouse. If this continues there will be a range of consequences including:

- melting of parts of the polar ice cap
- corresponding rises in sea levels, with the potential loss of much low-lying land, some of which is very densely populated
- increasing areas of desert, reducing the area of land easily available for cultivation
- changes in flora and fauna – in Britain, some of our existing upland species of plant and animals could disappear, but crops currently found only much further south in Europe might become a viable crop in our country because of the hotter environment
- increasing scarcity of drinking water in areas where the climate becomes significantly warmer
- significantly increased turbulence in the world's weather patterns, with much more extreme weather (the increase in the number of severe storms in Britain in recent years may well be a symptom of this effect).

There has been an increase in the burning of coal and oil since the end of World War II and it is the burning of coal, oil and petrol that accounts for much atmospheric pollution. The combination of increased fuel requirements and use of the car accounts in very large part for the increase in the concentration of carbon dioxide.

Think of ways in which the greenhouse effect will have an impact on the general life-styles of many people around the world if it extends its influence very much further.

### The hole in the ozone layer

Chlorofluorocarbons (or CFCs) have been identified as the gases responsible for the destruction of the ozone layer since the 1980s. Although ozone as part of our immediate atmosphere is a dangerous form of pollution caused by the interaction of sunlight on hydrocarbons and nitrogen oxides, there is a natural 'shield' of the gas around the outer atmosphere. This has always played a major role in reducing the level of ultra-violet light from the sun that reaches the Earth's surface. Scientists have found 'holes' in the ozone layer, particularly in the Arctic and Antarctic areas which reveal the extent and global nature of pollution. An increase in the amount of ultra-violet light has two effects:

- it increases the risk of sunburn
- which, in turn, increases the level of skin cancer.

Make sure that you understand the difference between the greenhouse effect and the hole in the ozone layer – they are not the same thing.

### Acid rain

This phenomenon is the result of air pollution and occurs when oxides of sulphur and nitrogen combine with moisture in the atmosphere to form sulphuric and nitric acids, which might then be blown hundreds of miles by the wind before falling as precipitation (rain, snow or fog).

In the early 1990s Britain had the highest percentage of trees damaged by acid rain of any country on Earth – 67 per cent was one estimate. At the same time, 80 per cent of the lakes in southern Norway had no fish, and neighbouring Sweden had an estimated 20,000 acidified lakes – these Scandinavian countries being primarily affected by pollution originating in more industrialised countries like the United Kingdom.

The countries of the world realise that the atmosphere has become increasingly polluted, and that the temperature of the world is going up.

Until recently, the full impact of global warming was not appreciated (or even accepted) by some. However, world governments are now taking steps to address pollution, but is it too late?

Pollution is a global concern, affecting countries that do not create much pollution themselves – global warming, acid rain and the developing holes in the ozone layer, for example, affect very wide areas.

## Water pollution

| AQA A | M2 |
| AQA B | M3 |
| EDEXCEL | M2 |
| OCR | M2 |

In addition to the pollution caused by acid rain, there is the direct pollution of the water in rivers, lakes and seas by contamination from micro-organisms, chemicals, industrial or other wastes and untreated sewage.

### Crop spraying

One common result of farmers spraying crops with nutrients is that, as part of the water cycle, a proportion of them will get washed into water courses. A river or stream that is full of bright green vegetation might look very healthy, but in reality these aquatic plants are depleting the water of the dissolved oxygen – which has the effect of killing other life, such as fish, that live in the river.

The ethical dilemma here is that farmers spray their fields in order to increase food yields from crops, which in turn means more food is available and at the cheapest possible prices. However, is this a price worth paying if we are, in effect, turning the countryside into an unnatural habitat sustained by chemical sprays with unwanted secondary effects? Should we always seek to produce the cheapest possible food, or do other considerations – such as caring for the wider environment – need to be taken into account?

*Is paying more for food in order to help protect the environment only an option for the wealthy who can afford it, or does the Earth need long-term protection and therefore more expensive food?*

### Pollution of the seas

The seas are also becoming polluted, for example:

* major oil spills from tankers have caused ecological disasters around the world
* the dumping of raw sewage just below the low-tide mark continues, although the European Union is working to end this practice. Pressure groups such as Surfers Against Sewage have campaigned for several years, and it is to be hoped that such dumping will soon be a thing of the past.

However, dealing with these issues raises other dilemmas:

* the effective treatment of sewage has seen water bills spiral upwards for domestic users, including those who struggle to make ends meet. Water is a necessity of life and yet people find themselves having to pay ever bigger bills, with the risk of having their supply cut off if they don't pay

*We would cut our petrol consumption if the maximum speed limit was cut to 50 mph – is this a viable proposition?*

* with regard to oil spills, it is clearly the case that as the world's demand for fuel continues to escalate, and the number of cars in use grows at a rapid rate, the amount of petrol being conveyed around the world will continue to increase. If we cut our use of petrol we could reverse this trend, but given our love-affair with the car, is this ever likely to happen?

## Genetically modified (GM) foods

| AQA A | M2 |
| AQA B | M1, M3 |
| EDEXCEL | M2 |
| OCR | M2 |

Currently the use of GM food is much more widespread and accepted in the United States than in Europe. It has been suggested that this is, in large part, because of the BSE scare in Europe, which created a scare about what was perceived as 'interfering with nature'. The main crops to be genetically modified are soya and

Genetically modified foods are produced as a result of scientists changing elements of a plant's genetic make-up – for example, removing genes that are susceptible to disease, or which limit a plant's ability to grow in a particular climate.

tomatoes, although in Britain there was such a reaction against GM food in 1999 that many supermarket chains and food manufacturers withdrew all food containing GM products from sale. This reaction was fuelled by the suggestion that evidence that genetically modified potato fed to experimental rats led to them developing brain tumours had been deliberately suppressed.

The main arguments for and against GM foods are shown in Table 9.2.

*Table 9.2 Arguments for and against GM foods*

| Pro-GM Foods | Anti-GM Foods |
| --- | --- |
| They can be made disease- and pest-resistant, so insecticide sprays, etc. are not needed. | Thorough laboratory testing has not been carried out. |
| Modification could make a crop viable in a climate where it is likely to fail in natural conditions. | Evidence of one set of experiments at least, has shown some development of cancers in rats fed GM potato. |
| The principle is the same as the selective breeding of animals, which has gone on for centuries. | Large areas containing only one type of GM crop will decimate natural habitats of wildlife and destroy ecosystems. |
| Big increases in yield could help put an end to hunger in the world. | It is not known whether the long-term effects of GM foods might be to create new strains of illness to which there might be no known cure. |

The manipulation of human genes has cultural and ideological, as well as ethical concerns – it is considered in the next chapter.

**KEY POINT**

GM food is much more widespread and accepted in the USA – in the soya bean crop, in particular, a large percentage of the total is now genetically modified.

In the UK there has been considerable concern about the subject of GM food, although much of the debate has been conducted at an emotional level.

Many European supermarkets have withdrawn products containing genetically modified elements.

Some who oppose GM foods are calling not so much for a blanket and permanent ban, but for an end for field trials until laboratory experiments can show that there will be no major environmental or health repercussions from developing GM foods.

## The use of nuclear power for generating electricity

AQA A  M2
AQA B  M1, M2
EDEXCEL  M2
OCR  M2

There has always been public concern about the various nuclear power stations situated around the world – although in reality only a minority of countries have the technology and resources to build such plants. This concern arises from the fact that the by-products of producing such hazardous fuel sources remain potentially dangerous for thousands of years. However, the reality is that *dramatically* more lives have been lost in the process of obtaining coal and oil for use in traditional power stations. The source of public concern is therefore the *potential* for disaster – and the evidence that when things go wrong the effects can be very severe over a very wide area. Consider the facts about the nuclear accident at Chernobyl in the Ukraine in April 1986:

- An explosion resulting from human error in one of the four reactors blew the top off the reactor.

- The design of the plant failed to meet modern, Western safety standards – in particular, the reactor was not housed in a separate containment building, and so escaping radioactive material was sent directly into the atmosphere.

- The core of the reactor was on fire and burning at 1,500°C, with radiation escaping in a huge plume that was dispersed by winds over much of northern Europe. In the UK, heavy rain falling over north Wales washed considerable amounts of radioactivity into the grass and soil, which affected sheep eating the grass to the extent that over a decade later some sheep still contained too much radiation to be sold for meat.

Can you imagine the logistics of this in a heavily populated area like Western Europe!

- 135,000 Ukrainians in a 1,000 mile radius of the Chernobyl plant had to be evacuated. There were at least 30 immediate deaths, but in subsequent years there has been a huge increase in people with cancers and in the number of children born with major disabilities.

There is an additional potential concern – that the uranium produced in the process of nuclear generation is of 'weapons grade'. If this fell into the hands of countries or groups who wished to make some kind of nuclear weapon (however primitive), the outcome could be catastrophic.

## Renewable energy sources

These are sources that are not finite and that can be used permanently without creating pollution. They fall into three main areas – water, wind and solar – and technology is being developed to generate electricity from all three (although at the moment they can produce only a small part of the global requirement for electricity).

### Water

Hydro-electric generation: turbines being turned by fast-flowing water channelled through pipes into power stations.

Generation from the flow of tides and waves: this currently requires a considerable area of water to generate a small amount of electricity.

### Wind

Wind turbines: these are increasingly common – especially in 'wind farms' where collections of often very large windmills can dominate a landscape. They can be visually very intrusive, and are noisy, with the result that they are more common in less densely populated areas – especially in countries like the United States. In the UK good examples can be seen in parts of mid-Wales, where there are lightly populated, hilly areas that are ideal for making maximum use of the wind.

### Solar

Solar panels: widely used around the world, these turn the sun's heat into electricity either for immediate use, or to charge batteries which can then supply power during periods when the sun is not shining. They are most effective in areas of the world with hot and sunny climates.

> Many of the developments in science and technology that have helped to give us an enhanced standard of living over the last half century have also created various forms of pollution which are harming the environment. We are now more aware of this – but are we doing enough to address the problems? We should also consider whether the advanced economies of the world will ever genuinely help poorer countries to gain a greater level of equality if this might also have the effect of increasing world pollution levels.

**KEY POINT**

## Progress check

1 What is the 'greenhouse effect'?

2 Name the main benefits that are claimed by supporters of genetically modified foods.

3 Explain two characteristics of renewable energy sources.

3 Renewable energy sources are not finite and can be used permanently without creating pollution.

2 Resistance to pests; ability to grow a crop over a wider area; much larger yields; less susceptible to plant diseases.

1 The process where 'greenhouse gases' – carbon dioxide in particular – allows the sun's rays to penetrate the atmosphere, but doesn't allow an equivalent heat loss, so that the temperature of the Earth is slowly rising.

# Sample question and model answer

Could it be argued reasonably that pollution will pose the biggest threat to the world in the coming years?

**Step 1**
Introduction – define 'pollution'.

*Pollution refers to the contamination of the Earth's air and water with by-products from industry, mineral extraction, domestic usage and vehicle emissions. Ever since early peoples burned wood for cooking and warmth there has been some form of pollution. However, today the Earth has:*

- *a population of six billion people*

It is this aspect that the answer needs to concentrate on.

- *industrial and technological processes now create potentially dangerous by-products to a far greater extent than has happened in the past.*

*Arguments that pollution could well pose the biggest threat to the world might include:*

**Step 2**
A balanced answer will need to consider both sides of the argument.

- *Industry is putting a deadly mixture of polluting chemicals into the atmosphere.*
- *Emissions from vehicles of various kinds, including aircraft, are being blamed for an already large increase in serious respiratory disorders.*
- *The nuclear industry has already had a series of potentially catastrophic accidents such as that at Chernobyl. With problems over the long-term storage of nuclear waste still not fully resolved, the industry is a possible source of very major future accidents.*
- *The results of the greenhouse effect could have major impacts on the lives of millions – such as people having to evacuate low-lying areas. Such pressures could fuel future conflicts, put pressure on food supplies, etc.*

*On the other hand it could be pointed out that:*

- *There have been potentially catastrophic situations throughout the course of history – war, famine, disease, etc. The situation we are now facing is no graver than some of these in the past – which did not prove to be catastrophic.*
- *Pressures caused by other factors, particularly the rise in the world's population, pose a far greater threat to human survival, unless we can start to feed the world more effectively.*
- *Without doubt we have created more pollution in recent years than ever before, but now the seriousness of this (and its potential long-term effects) has been appreciated, work can be done to reduce both the amounts of pollution and its worst effects.*
- *At the height of the Industrial Revolution there were examples of localised pollution that was probably greater than current levels – yet when the industry that caused this ceased to function, the ecosystems recovered in quite a short time in most cases.*

**Step 3**
Do not be afraid to state a personal viewpoint in your conclusion.

*You might reach an equally valid conclusion on either side of the debate – or even take an 'agnostic' viewpoint and say it is too early to say the extent to which pollution might be the biggest problem facing the world. However, a conclusion must always be based on the points you have previously brought up, not on new points raised for the first time. For example:*

It is clear that the Earth is currently facing unprecedented pressure, both from a population perspective as the global population reaches 6 billion and from the degree of pollution being emitted from all kinds of sources but in particular from industrial, domestic and vehicular sources. However, the Earth has in the past shown itself to be resilient and on sites previously decimated by the heavy industry of previous times nature quickly reasserts itself when given the opportunity. Aided by a realisation of the scale of the problem, government, scientists and industrialists are now working to address the major causes of potential catastrophe. It would not be wise to underestimate the scale of the problem, but at the same time humanity has always sought

## Sample question and model answer (continued)

to overcome its major problems and is not yet ready to press the suicide button. Set alongside the continuing difficulties in preserving world peace and managing the rise in the global population it would be wrong to assert pollution constitutes the biggest threat facing the world today.

## Practice examination questions

### Short answer questions

1 How has the development of satellite technology been of practical use to humanity?

2 Where are the potential dangers in the process of nuclear-power generation?

3 How has domestic entertainment been transformed through technological developments over the last century?

### Essay question

4 What are the main arguments advanced for *and* against the use of genetically modified food?

# Chapter 10

# Science and culture

*The following topics are covered in this chapter:*

- *Science in a cultural context*
- *Some contemporary controversies*

## 10.1 Science in a cultural context

*After studying this section you should be able to:*

- *define the meaning of the terms: technology, science, culture and ideology*
- *outline key developments in the philosophy of science*

### Defining terms

| | |
|---|---|
| AQA A | M2 |
| AQA B | M1, M2, M3 |
| EDEXCEL | M2 |
| OCR | M2 |

The inductive theories are based on the idea that because something has been shown to happen, it will *always* happen – although this cannot be *proved* to be the case for the future, only for the past.

Before discussing the main issues in this chapter, it will help to begin by looking at some basic definitions.

**Technology** is 'The study or use of applied science and mechanical arts.' In other words, it is the putting into practical use of the ideas derived from scientists and others. Technologists are essentially the practical people who put advances made by others into practical use.

**Science** is 'The branch of knowledge conducted on objective principles involving systematised observation of, and experiment with, phenomena, especially those concerned with the material and the functions of the physical universe.' As we have seen in Chapter 8, the scientist seeks to be empirical and objective, and to claim as being true only what can be observed and tested. However, because science is largely based on inductive theories it cannot be claimed to be inherently 'true'. Scientific methodology, and its discoveries, have however made great strides over the last century and there is no reason to suppose that this will not continue.

**Culture** can be defined as: 'The customs, civilisation and achievement of a particular time or people. The arts and other manifestations of human intellectual achievement regarded collectively.' Much Western culture is based on its Christian tradition. At one time most of its art, music and literature was dominated by religion and even though organised Christianity no longer retains such dominance its philosophy still underpins our culture. It is perhaps in the area of culture that there are the greatest tensions resulting from advances in technology and science – because the latter now enable humanity to enter into activities once thought to be the realm of God alone.

**Ideology** refers to 'The system of ideas that lies at the heart of an economic or political theory at the macro level, or the manner of thinking of a social class or individual.' Many people might form the idea that someone was from a certain class because of the way they speak or dress, for example. However, this is simply an idea and is obviously not based on the kind of objective and experimental basis used by the scientist to determine facts. This doesn't mean that such ideas aren't important, because we all live in societies and communities and will to some extent be coloured by the views and aspirations of that society. Indeed, certain ideologies might lead to scientific study being concentrated on a particular sector or direction – at the height of the Cold War between the West and the Communist bloc it was clear that scientific and technological developments in areas like the Space Race, or weapons technology were very much inspired by the need to assert the 'superiority' of the ideological basis of one side over the other.

> Although technology and science have a very different methodology and technique, they are still strongly influenced by the culture and ideology of the background from which they come.
>
> **KEY POINT**

## The philosophy of science

AQA A — M2
AQA B — M1
EDEXCEL — M2
OCR — M2

The philosophy of science concerns the study of the ultimate nature of existence, reality and knowledge, and is as old as the study of science itself – perhaps particularly in the area of Physics. The earliest philosophers of science to commit their thoughts to writing were found in Ancient Greece. The theories of Aristotle, for example, lay at the very heart of much scientific thinking right through to the origins of the modern scientific world, and the work and writing of people like Galileo.

From around the sixteenth century we can see an attempt to bring a mathematical objectivity to scientific thought. This developed more strongly in the following century with the work of scientists/philosophers like Descartes, and continued with the work of people like Sir Isaac Newton, whose thinking extended beyond our own Earth into seeking to explain the rationale behind the universe. This process has continued through to modern science in, for example, the work of Albert Einstein on relativity, or the work of physicists developing concepts around the theory of quantum mechanics.

### Science and God

Science does not prove or disprove the existence of some form of divine being.

Particularly in the twentieth century the idea developed that there was somehow a clash between science and God – that one had to support one side against the other. However, it is unlikely that any scientist would see it as part of their role to prove or disprove the existence of God – although over time various philosophical 'proofs' have been put forward seeking to either show or deny the existence of a deity. For example, Newton's work on the nature of the universe and on gravity was taken as evidence that there was a divine being, since it suggested there was order in the universe – which, it was said, could only have come about as a result of direct creation. It is nonetheless true that scientific developments *have* affected our ethics and our sense of morality, as we shall see later in this chapter.

There has been interplay between science and ethical aspects of culture and ideology for a long time.

While Newton's work was in the physical sciences, the influence of ethical judgements can also be seen in the life sciences. There are sometimes violent arguments about the use of animals in experiments, which have been going on for at least a century. In the nineteenth century, for example, Jeremy Bentham (the Utilitarian thinker) was concerned about the extent to which moral consideration should apply to animals and was sensitive to their treatment. He claimed the pertinent question was whether animals could suffer – and in concluding that they could, he felt that they should therefore be bound by moral considerations.

A Utilitarian believed that it was important to seek the greatest possible good for the greatest possible number.

Also in the field of life science is the scientific theory that has perhaps had the most immediate impact on the moral perspective of our society – that concerning evolution as put forward in Charles Darwin's *On the Origin of Species* in 1859. From this came the idea that morality has merely been the result of certain habits acquired by humanity in the course of evolution. Such thought caused great shock to a culture that had accepted as literal truth the phrase in the Bible's book of Genesis which said that man was made in God's image.

'Superman' – an individual who would create a new master morality based on objectivity, not on the support of the weak masses (who sought self-protection through morality).

A startling, but logical, development from this idea was that put forward by the German philosopher, Nietzsche (1844–1900), who claimed that moral conduct is only needed by the weak – that moral conduct is a mechanism that allows the weak to hold back the self-realisation of the strong. He wrote of the development of the 'superman', and by the 1930s this idea was embroiled in Nazi political philosophy, with its concepts of the 'master race'.

Cloning is the process of manipulating a fragment of the DNA of a plant or animal so that identical copies of the molecule are reproduced, which can generate into a full replica of the original. Dolly, the sheep, is perhaps the best example to date.

The work of scientists is sometimes put under limits by cultural and ideological considerations.

The scientist, basing work so far as is possible on objective experimentation and mathematical principles, does perhaps need to apply ethical considerations at the same time. Recent work in embryology and genetic modification, especially the idea of cloning, has very clear ethical dimensions and a Royal Commission under Baroness Warnock looked into this. If ethics is based on standards of human behaviour there are clear cultural and ideological undertones for the work of scientists and technologists. For example, doctors in hospitals now use a range of modern technology to keep alive premature, or sick babies, but in Ancient Greece it was considered morally right to put such babies to death. Scientists are therefore likely to be bound by questions like, 'When is an act right?', 'When is an experiment justifiable?' and 'What is the nature of good and bad?', even though in different societies and at different times the answers to these questions might not be the same.

> **KEY POINT**
>
> While scientists base much of their work on objective experimentation and observation, the ideas and cultural norms of society in which they work may change – indeed, this change may be led by scientific development. Nevertheless, society can still apply ethical constraints to what it considers to be the proper boundaries for science, as is seen in the arguments around issues such as cloning.

## Progress check

1 In what way does technology develop from science?

2 What is the name given to a system of ideas that lies at the heart of the economic or political theory of a country, a social class or an individual?

3 Give an example of technological advances being accelerated by the desire of rival ideologies to prove superiority over the other.

4 Which English scientist sought to detail a rationality for the universe in his work during the seventeenth century?

5 What areas of contemporary scientific controversy were examined by the Royal Commission chaired by Baroness Warnock?

1 It puts ideas developed from scientists into practical use.
2 Ideology.
3 The one example is that of the Space Race between the US and the Soviet Union.
4 Sir Isaac Newton.
5 Embryology and genetic modification.

# 10.2 Some contemporary controversies

*After studying this section you should be able to:*

● *describe the opposing characteristics of science & technology and culture & ideology*
● *present arguments for and against a number of controversial ethical issues in the field of science and technology*

*LEARNING SUMMARY*

## Are science and technology in opposition to culture and ideology

| AQA A | M2 |
| AQA B | M1 |
| EDEXCEL | M2 |
| OCR | M2 |

The question in the title of this section lies at the heart of this chapter and could form a part of General Studies' exams.

The basis of science and technology is that it:

● is objective and based on observation and measurement (with technology being the logical and practical developments often arising from scientific work)
● attempts to remove any preconceptions, or pre-judgement of outcomes
● expects results that would be the same wherever and whenever experiments are conducted

- is not directly concerned about outcomes of work being done.

On the other hand, culture and ideology is:

- rooted in the past traditions of a particular society or community
- likely to show important differences in perceptions, practice and morality in different geographical areas
- likely to change over time in response to changing circumstances
- not limited by what can be observed and quantified – for example, much culture is based on a religious background – and the existence of any kind of divine is not provable.

If, on the one hand, technology and science is based on the present and looking towards developments into the future, while on the other hand culture and ideology is based on the present, but is rooted in the past, then it could be said that they are pulling in opposite directions. A scientist who wanted to undertake some research using foetal tissue (that is, tissue which has been taken from a dead foetus) might well feel that their objective work was being severely curtailed, if not forbidden, by the society in which they lived.

However, it can also be argued that culture and ideology is not fixed in time, but is responsive to changing situations and to developments. Many changes and developments are brought about by science and technology and so it is likely that culture and ideology will respond – albeit not as rapidly as some scientists and technologists would like. Over a long period of time, such social adaptation in response to scientific developments can be dramatic. For example:

**1000** AD People in Europe thought the Earth was flat, that heaven was above the stars and hell was below the Earth.

**1500** AD It had been shown that the Earth was round, but it was still felt that heaven was a physical place somewhere beyond what could be observed.

**2000** AD Space research has found no physical evidence of a divine being, or state of eternity. Modern theology stresses the spiritual nature of the divine, but science has not disproved the existence of a divinity.

The last point arguably demonstrates a culture and ideology that is not opposed to developments in technology and science. This model would seem to fit with the idea of our being a liberal society which is open to change and receptive to new ideas. However, a society dominated by conservative and reactionary forces (in the past such examples have been provided by various religions or political ideologies) is far more likely to be resistant to change, since it is wedded to its ideology being fundamentally correct or 'true'. In such circumstances culture and ideology might well find themselves in opposition to new ideas in technology and science.

> It is areas of controversy like these that examiners may well seek to test your understanding and ability to argue a particular viewpoint.

**KEY POINT**

Science and technology, and culture and ideology are coming from different perspectives. Science and technology looks to expand our knowledge and use of the world in which we live, while culture and ideology give us a way to behave and a code in which to operate our lives which is based on 'where we have come from' over time. However, although different, they are not necessarily in opposition.

Science is seeking to be objective, and to put forward a system based on observation and measurement. Culture and ideology are much more flexible, and change over time. Out thinking may be part of our culture and ideology, but this is not objective information in a scientific sense.

## Genetic engineering

| | |
|---|---|
| AQA A | M2 |
| AQA B | M1, M2 |
| EDEXCEL | M2 |
| OCR | M2 |

This is the process of changing the inherited characteristics of an organism in a predetermined way by altering elements of its genetic material. Gene therapy is an important area of medical advance with many applications, some of which bring up cultural and ideological issues.

- Functional genes are provided to cells lacking that function in order to correct a genetic disorder of acquired disease. Some hereditary diseases have in the past not been treatable, and in some cases have had extremely serious effects. One example is Huntington's Chorea – a disease of the brain that starts in early middle age, leading to uncontrollable body movements ('chorea' means dance), loss of memory and eventual profound personality change. Since adults do not develop the disease until after the age when many of them will have had children they may already have passed on the faulty gene by the time they know they have the illness. Being able to correct this faulty gene holds out the hope of treatment in the future.

- In some cases where it is known that a parent has a genetic illness a genetic counsellor can work with a couple to discuss possible consequences of a pregnancy and often tests can be carried out on the foetus. If it is clear that a child will be born with a serious disability a women can be offered an abortion.

- Some people object to both uses for gene therapy outlined above, largely due to religious belief that God creates life and it is not part of humanity's role to interfere with this. There are also concerns that such medical procedures are only a step away from the Nazi ideal of the creation of a 'master-race'.

- Genetic engineering is already being used to create insulin (used in the treatment of diabetes) and in the creation of Factor 8, the clotting agent in blood which is needed by haemophiliacs.

- Genetic engineering has led to the development of 'cloning' – in essence, the process of manipulating a DNA fragment so that multiple copies of an identical molecule can be made. Dolly the sheep hit the headlines when she was created in an Edinburgh laboratory from cells taken from her mother. The major arguments here hinge around the morality of developing human cloning if it becomes possible. Current work in this field is concentrating on the targeting of specific tissues for direct treatment, or on the removal of tissue so that therapeutic genes can be added in a lab prior to the return of the treated cells to the patient.

> An example of a technique considered inappropriate for development by society.

Another possible area that is currently regarded as unacceptable is work on changing the fundamental structure of a sperm or egg so that there is a permanent genetic change. This could lead to, for example, 'designer babies' – people seeking to have only children who are geniuses, or with some other desired attribute. This, again, can with some justification be seen as a step towards the master-race, whilst the treatment of specific faulty genes can be compared with the process of organ transplantation.

> **KEY POINT**
>
> Gene therapy is an important area of medical and scientific development.
>
> However, some people object to it on the grounds that it allows humans to 'play God' (a view not held by all people with religious convictions).
>
> There are tough ethical arguments to consider in looking at how far genetic engineering should go.

## Euthanasia

| | |
|---|---|
| AQA A | M2 |
| AQA B | M1 |
| EDEXCEL | M2 |
| OCR | M2 |

> There are a variety of moral judgements to be made here – think about what they are.

In Britain it is illegal to assist another person to die – this applies to ordinary people as well as to doctors with patients who are terminally ill. However, while this may seem to be clear cut there are several areas where understanding the culture and ethics of society would be helpful in clarifying what actually constitutes helping somebody to die.

- To set out to kill someone is clearly murder, but what about when somebody is in a permanent vegetative state (PVS) and might remain that way for years until they die and the doctor orders the life-support machine to be switched off – this prematurely allows the person to die.

- What if someone is terminally ill and likely to be in great pain prior to their death? If that person signed a declaration (at a time when they were still considered capable of making a rational decision) that they would like their life to be terminated before their final demise, would a doctor who carried out their patient's request be guilty of murder? Is reducing a patient to a state of total drug dependency as the only means of controlling pain before death any more moral than giving them a dose big enough to send them to a peaceful death?

In Britain, the Voluntary Euthanasia Society was established in 1935 to campaign for the legalisation of euthanasia in certain circumstances. The law itself has not changed, but public opinion does seem to be changing and there have been several recent examples in Britain and abroad where doctors who had been charged with murder following allegations that they helped their patients to die have then been acquitted. The law in respect to euthanasia was originally based on the Christian belief that only God has the power to give or to take life. Most religions around the world oppose euthanasia, but if public opinion is softening it will be interesting to see if the law is at least modified or clarified in the next few years.

## Animal experimentation and animal rights

| AQA A | M2 |
| AQA B | M1, M3 |
| EDEXCEL | M2 |
| OCR | M2 |

Animals are used in biomedical and veterinary research to improve the health of both humans and other animals. Animals have been used in scientific research for at least a century and, as mentioned above, the nineteenth century philosopher Jeremy Bentham said that since animals could feel pain, humans had moral responsibilities towards them.

Supporters of animal experimentation have claimed that advances in medicine, for example in the fields of antibiotics and vaccines, have resulted from the use of animals in such work. Current work on the treatment of various cancers uses animals, and researchers hope this work will go on to help save many human lives in the future.

Legislation regulates the use of laboratory animals in research and education, and covers the treatment, housing and husbandry of laboratory animals, and the utilisation of possible alternatives to animals. Toxicity tests that used to be done by putting drops into the eyes of rabbits to text for reaction to soaps or cosmetics are no longer carried out in Britain and all licences for such work have been terminated.

If you answer a General Studies question on the morality of this work remember to remain objective, even if you hold strong personal views.

Opponents of animal experimentation will sometimes go to extreme lengths to try to stop testing. Several individual researchers and various laboratories have needed police protection against opponents of their work using animals. Such opponents claim that society has not given scientists permission for animal experimentation – and take the view that since animals cannot themselves defend what they see as the rights of animals, then direct action by humans on their behalf is justified in seeking to end experiments or to 'liberate' animals.

Pro-hunt supporters claim evidence that hunting tends to capture the older and sick animals, thus improving the 'blood stock' of those left – in effect, helping along natural selection by some human intervention.

Animals have been used for human sport and entertainment for many centuries. Society no longer finds bull and badger baiting, or dog or cock fighting acceptable, but still allows fox and stag hunting. Scientific studies of the effects of hunting on stags has led the National Trust to ban the hunting of these animals on its land, and attempts are being made to bring in legislation to ban all hunting with hounds.

Supporters of both sides of the argument about fox hunting claim to be supported by scientific evidence and perhaps at the end of the day it will be cultural considerations that will win the day. Opinion polls have shown consistently in recent years that a sizeable majority are opposed to hunting with dogs.

When zoos were first opened they were clearly for entertainment. Have they now sought a more realistic basis for existence – or are they trying to find an 'excuse' to stay open?

Another issue that causes controversy is the keeping of animals in circuses and zoos – is this merely a form of public entertainment or are zoos, in particular, correct when they claim a scientific basis for their work? They say that educational, zoological and conservation benefits arise from their work – although opponents point out that animals are often kept in unsuitable housing, lack space and live in an unnatural habitat and climate.

In the UK, experiments on live animals are allowed under tightly controlled conditions in licensed laboratories. This is clearly set out in legislation.

Supporters of animal experimentation believe it is the most effective way of making medical advances, particularly in areas where there is currently no known cure.

Opponents believe that humans have no right to carry out experiments on animals – and that animals have rights just as humans do. They point out that often there are alternatives to animal experiments, and these should be further developed. They also point out that humans might not have the same reaction to a drug as animals in a laboratory.

## Medical ethics

| AQA A | M2 |
|-------|----|
| AQA B | M1 |
| EDEXCEL | M2 |
| OCR | M2 |

These areas of controversy that involve science in pushing and extending the boundaries of culture and acceptability are only a few examples. You should try to think of others and the arguments they generate.

We have already mentioned some ethical problems concerned with medical research that stretch the boundaries of what society finds acceptable. These particularly concern human life itself – such as in the fields of genetics, embryology and investigations and processes that involve foetal material available after an abortion has been carried out. The culture of contemporary society now accepts 'test tube babies' – conception outside the womb – even though this technique is comparatively new and opponents see it as another example of doctors interfering with God's plans in nature.

However, there are other areas relating to pregnancy that many would feel uncomfortable with, or would oppose:

- In relation to the issue of surrogacy – a situation where a surrogate mother agreed to conceive and give birth to a child for a homosexual couple so they can bring it up as a family, would be clearly out of keeping with the Christian view of the family – and, indeed, society as a whole might not yet be ready to accept such a practice.

- In relation to the use of embryos for research – currently this can be done for the first 14 days of an embryo's 'life' whilst it is still simple cells that have no specific functions in the developing foetus (for example, being the forerunner of eyes, heart or limbs). It is argued that such an embryo cannot be equated with a human life – it is merely a collection of cells without a nervous system that can feel no pleasure, pain or other feelings. British law allows for this and evidence suggests that it has the support of a majority. However, some holders of religious beliefs, perhaps Roman Catholics most vociferously, oppose this and say that since those cells will develop into human life then to terminate the embryo's existence is the same as murdering one of God's creatures – and that *all* life that will be human is sacred.

There is considerable controversy over developments and experimentation in the fields of embryology and genetics.

Some say the law must be strengthened in areas where new medical technology has developed, and the law is unclear. They believe doctors are meddling with creation.

Others say that such attitudes stifle medical and scientific progress – and that work that is seen as controversial today will one day be seen as routine. They claim that such work will enable the better treatment of a range of genetic diseases, help counter infertility and enable a far deeper understanding of human health and effectiveness.

## Progress check

1 What type of research is leading to advances in the treatment of some hereditary diseases?

2 What name is given to the process by which a fragment of DNA material is manipulated so that it reproduces itself, and potentially could carry on doing so?

3 What body was formed in 1935 to campaign for changes in the law that states that it must always be illegal to assist another person to end their life, even if they are terminally ill?

4 What are two fundamental objections to the carrying out of abortions?

5 What type of testing using live animals is no longer licensed to be carried out in Britain?

1 Gene therapy.
2 Cloning.
3 Voluntary Euthanasia Society.
4 (i) It is interfering with God's creation.
(ii) Life begins at conception – so abortion is the destruction of an unborn child.
5 Toxicity tests, usually for soaps and cosmetics, that involved putting drops into the eyes of rabbits.

## Sample question and model answer

What are the arguments put forward by scientists who use animals in their work, and how might they be countered by those who oppose such experimentation?

**Step 1**
Establish the areas in which animal experimentation is used.

*You might begin with an introduction like that given below:*

Animal experimentation is used in medicine to improve human health. Major advances have been claimed, and work continues in such fields as cures for cancers. However, there are ethical objections, and sometimes faulty conclusions are drawn – Thalidomide being a classic example of a drug tested on animals, but then had catastrophic results when used on humans.

**Step 2**
Set out the arguments, remembering to be objective even if you hold strong personal opinions.

*In favour of animal experimentation:*

- *Animals are bred in captivity specially for experiments – they have not therefore had lives in the world outside the lab.*
- *Tight laws and regulations govern the treatment of animals, and it is in the scientist's interests to look after them since a premature death might mean that no results would be obtained.*

Examiners will not welcome purely emotional arguments about 'poor little bunnies'.

- *The lives of animals and of humans cannot be seen as being equal – if human lives can be saved, the loss of a few animals is a justifiable sacrifice.*
- *It would not be acceptable to test drugs on humans until the trial stage, and only then on volunteers.*
- *If a member of your family had a fatal disease that could be cured by a new treatment developed from animal experimentation would you not be grateful for such treatments?*

*Against animal experimentation:*

- *Animals have rights that need to be protected – it is arrogant of humanity to assume a superiority that allows the exploitation of animals.*
- *Computer simulations, and other new techniques, can replace the need for much experimentation.*
- *Many experiments that are carried out are repeats, merely to keep reconfirming the first results – this is totally unnecessary.*
- *Because a drug may have no side-effects on an animal it cannot be assumed that this will be the case in humans – as mentioned in the introduction, Thalidomide is a classic example of this.*

**Step 3**
Conclusion. Having set out your arguments for both sides you can now draw them together and express a personal opinion.

*An example of a conclusion is as follows:*

Some people clearly believe that the breeding of animals simply for use in experiments, some of which might inflict pain, suffering and ultimate death, is not acceptable even for rats. However, if human lives can be saved and cures found for illnesses that are currently fatal I believe the sacrifice of animal life is justified. The pain, anguish and grief of a terminally ill person is shared by the family and often a wider community. This is not the case with animals, and if the ultimate result of animal experimentation is to help preserve and extend human health and happiness the work of scientists is morally and scientifically justified.

# Practice examination questions

## Short answer questions

*1* How might you define 'science' and 'ideology'?

*2* How could gene therapy be of use in the treatment of some diseases?

*3* Why does abortion arouse so much moral outrage in some people's eyes?

## Essay question

*4* Are technology and science inherently opposed to culture and ideology?

# Chapter 11

# Mathematical reasoning

*The following topics are covered in this chapter:*

- *The application of number in General Studies*
- *Areas on which you might be tested*

## 11.1 The application of number in General Studies

*After studying this section you should be able to:*

- *explain why application of number is a part of the General Studies examination syllabus*
- *describe what key skills are and list all those required in order to gain the key skills qualification for post-16 students*

LEARNING SUMMARY

### Key skills in General Studies

| AQA A | M2 |
|---|---|
| AQA B | M3 |
| EDEXCEL | M2 |
| OCR | M2 |

Application of number is a compulsory element of all General Studies AS exams.

The **application of number** forms a compulsory part of all General Studies specifications – so if you do not like mathematics as a subject, the sad news is it cannot be escaped! However, in General Studies what is required is not simply the ability to solve mathematical problems, it is much more the ability to use and apply the skills you will have been taught earlier in your academic career.

However, this is not the only area that is compulsory if an examination board is to get its General Studies course approved – the quality of **written communication** also has to be taken into account. However, since this can be done as part of the process of marking every candidate's essays, this does not have to form a separate part of the examination that can be clearly identified – as is the case with the application of number.

There is a very good reason why the application of number and the quality of written communication need to be addressed specifically. General Studies, in common with other AS and A Level courses, have to be able to contribute towards the gaining of the **key skills qualification** that has been developed for all post-16 students. There are six areas of key skills:

| | |
|---|---|
| Application of number | Improving own learning |
| Communication | Working with others |
| Information technology | Problem solving |

The first three skills are assessed for the National Qualification in Key Skills, and it is these that AS and A Level courses need to be able to address if your General Studies course is going to lead you to an AS or A Level. You will have to be assessed on the application of number and the quality of your written communication.

All the exam boards will therefore be asking you specific questions on the application of number as part of your AS Level examination. At the same time, your school or college might well have chosen General Studies as the way to deliver *all six* areas of the key skills framework.

As a part of your AS Level exam you will be asked questions that seek to demonstrate how well you can apply your ability to use number based on skills you should have already acquired.

KEY POINT

# 11.2 Areas on which you might be tested

LEARNING SUMMARY

**After studying this section you should be able to:**

- *cite the various subject areas on which you could be tested*
- *explain the basic terms and concepts involved in each area*

The following areas are those which are set out in the different General Studies specifications, and about which questions might be set in the AS Level examination:

- **the layout of data sets**
- **amounts and sizes:** units, area, volume, diagrams, perimeter
- **scales and proportion:** axes, graphs, ratio, charts
- **statistics:** mean, median, mode, distribution, probability
- **formula:** percentages and rates, equations, sampling.

## Data sets

| | |
|---|---|
| AQA A | M2 |
| AQA B | M3 |
| EDEXCEL | M2 |
| OCR | M2 |

> Data has been defined as 'a group of known, given, or ascertained facts, from which inferences or a conclusion can be drawn, or on which a discussion can be based.'

KEY POINT

A data set is a way of setting out information in a way that makes analysis possible. Data can most easily be arranged into rows and columns so that information can be read off, or if you have been involved in collecting data as part of a survey you can more easily store the information you have acquired on computer. Table 11.1 illustrates the clarity that a data set can provide.

| Student | Faculty | Sex | A Level points | Degree class |
|---|---|---|---|---|
| 1 | A | F | 7 | 2.1 |
| 2 | EN | M | 3 | 2.2 |
| 3 | EN | M | 2 | Fail |
| 4 | ED | F | 5 | 2.2 |
| 5 | S | M | 2 | 2.1 |
| 6 | B | F | 6 | 2.1 |
| 7 | A | F | 8 | 2.1 |
| 8 | EN | M | 3 | 3 |
| 9 | EN | M | 3 | 3 |
| 10 | ED | M | * | 2.2 |

Key: A = Arts    B = Business    ED = Education    EN = Engineering
     S = Science    M = Male    F = Female    * = Missing data

*Table 11.1 Faculty, A Level points and degree classification of a sample of students*

Use of a data set in a General Studies exam.

In a General Studies exam you may well be presented with quite a large data set from which you will be asked to answer questions. The information you will require in order to answer will be contained within the data set. Some questions will be simply asking you to extract numerical information, others might ask you to write a paragraph on the topic covered in the table. You will gain marks not only for the quality of the analysis you have put forward, but also on the way you have used data from the data set to support your argument. Similarly, you might be asked to extract data to use in another form, such as in the creation of a bar graph, or pie chart.

## Amounts and sizes

| AQA A | M2 |
| AQA B | M3 |
| EDEXCEL | M2 |
| OCR | M2 |

This covers the subjects of units, area (including Pythagoras' Theorem) and volume.

### Units

This is simply defined as 'a standard used in the measurement of a physical quantity'.

Many General Studies' students may, for example, be familiar with the Department of Health's definitions of units of alcohol that can be consumed if an individual is to remain within safe limits of consumption. A unit is defined as being one glass of wine, a small glass (pub measure) of spirits or half a pint of beer – all are deemed to have the equivalent amount of alcohol and can therefore be measured against each other.

### Area

This is concerned with measurement of a surface. For a rectangle (which includes squares) you multiply two adjacent sides to find the area: see Figure 11.1.

4 cm x 2 cm
= 8 cm² (squared centimetres)

*Figure 11.1*

A triangle represents half a rectangle, and so can be calculated by dividing the length times the height by two – see Figure 11.2.

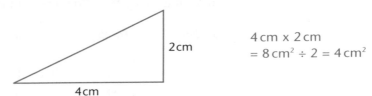

4 cm x 2 cm
= 8 cm² ÷ 2 = 4 cm²

*Figure 11.2*

### Pythagoras' Theorem

Where a triangle contains a right angle you can use Pythagoras' Theorem to determine the area – the square of the hypotenuse (the side opposite the right angle) is equal to sum of the squares of the other two sides – to work out the length of the third side – see Figure 11.3.

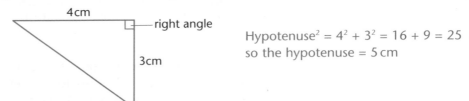

Hypotenuse² = 4² + 3² = 16 + 9 = 25
so the hypotenuse = 5 cm

*Figure 11.3*

Where a shape is irregular, such as **a trapezium**, it can be broken down into rectangles and triangles in order to find the area – see Figure 11.4. The ways set out above can then be used and the totals for the two triangles and the rectangle can be added to obtain the area.

*Figure 11.4*

The **area of a circle** is worked out by multiplying pi by the radius squared ($\pi \times r^2$) – see Figure 11.5.

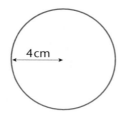

4 cm

a circle with 4 cm radius has an area:

pi x radius x radius
$= \pi \times 4 \times 4 = \pi \times 16$
$= 50.3$ cm.

*Figure 11.5*

## Volume

This is defined as the measure of extent in three-dimensional space. It might, for example, be the volume of water in a glass. It is calculated by multiplying length, width and breadth for cuboids (see Figure 11.6). Where an object is a prism (a solid which is exactly the same shape all the way through), the volume is the area of the cross section multiplied by the length (see Figure 11.7).

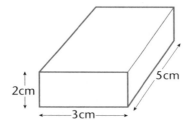

5 cm
2 cm
3 cm

The volume of a cuboid is the length x width x height.

In this illustration: 3 x 5 x 2 $= 30$ cm$^3$.

*Figure 11.6*

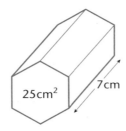

25 cm$^2$
7 cm

The volume of a prism or cylinder is the area of cross section x length.

In this illustration this is 25 x 7 $= 175$ cm$^3$.

*Figure 11.7*

## Perimeter

The word 'perimeter' is used to describe the length of a 'closed curve', i.e. one that is unbroken – for example, a circle (where there is no gap in the line making the curve).

## Scales and proportion

| AQA A | M2 |
|---|---|
| AQA B | M3 |
| EDEXCEL | M2 |
| OCR | M2 |

Whatever exam board you use, much of this will involve the use of graphs and charts.

### Graph

This is a diagram showing the relationship between two variable quantities, each measured along one of a pair of lines called an **axis**. Graphs are often used to show trends – for example, newspapers publish graphs showing the rise or fall in the fortunes of political parties as a proportion of the electorate that will vote for them over periods of time, or showing the fluctuations in the share price of a company over time. A graph is an excellent way of reflecting trends over a period. The same information could equally be provided in tabular form, but this does not provide the immediacy of looking at a graph. Information can also be extrapolated from a graph.

> To **extrapolate** means to calculate what is unknown by extending what is known – for example, by reading off information gathered from the line of a graph to gain additional information.

### Charts

These are sets of numbers in graphical form. They can take several forms.

#### Pictograms

A simple chart using symbols, each of which represents a certain quality. They are imprecise, but can give an immediate visual impression (see Figure 11.8).

#### Bar charts

A graph composed of a number of bars, either vertical or horizontal, with the same width. The length of the bars represents the number, or magnitude, of the quantity being illustrated (see Figure 11.9).

#### Pie charts

These show the relative number of different alternatives as the slices of a circle. They are clearest when the different sectors progressively decrease in size from largest to smallest as you go round the circle (see Figure 11.10).

= 10 lorries

*Figure 11.8 Pictogram showing the number of heavy lorries passing a survey point over a five-hour period*

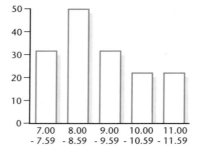

*Figure 11.9 Bar chart showing the number of heavy lorries passing a survey point over a five-hour period*

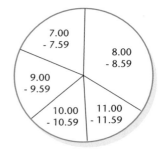

*Figure 11.10 Pie chart showing the number of heavy lorries passing a survey point over a five-hour period*

## Statistics

| AQA A | M2 |
|---|---|
| AQA B | M3 |
| EDEXCEL | M2 |
| OCR | M2 |

It is very easy to misuse the terminology of statistics. Each term has a specific meaning and you should be aware of the correct use of each.

> Make sure you know the difference between the terms 'mean', 'median' and 'mode'.

### Mean

The **mean** value is one that takes every value being considered into account. It is worked out by adding together all the numbers (values) that are being used and then dividing the total by the number of values involved.

e.g. To calculate the mean of the values 2 + 4 + 4 + 6 + 9 you should do the sum: 2 + 4 + 4 + 6 + 9 = 25. The number of values is 5 so divide 5 into 25. The mean is 5.

## Median

The **median** is the middle value of a group of values that have been arranged in order of size. It is useful to establish this when a group of values has some extraordinary values compared to the rest of the values, i.e. to minimise the effects of 'rogue scores' which could occur in any number set.

e.g. In the scores 8, 9, 10, 11, 12, 13, 84, the median is 11 (i.e. there are three values below it and three values above).

(If you worked out the *mean* for the same group of values, the total added together would be 150. Divided by the number of values (7), the mean = 21.)

## Mode

The **mode** of a group of scores is that most frequently occurring.

e.g. To find the mode of the following set of values: 6, 9, 7, 8, 6, 8, 7, 6, 8, 6, 7, 7, 8, 6, 9, 10, 7, 7, 6, 7, these could be tabulated:

| Value | 6 | 7 | 8 | 9 | 10 |
|---|---|---|---|---|---|
| Frequency | 5 | 8 | 4 | 2 | 1 |

It can then easily be seen that the number 7 is the mode – or modal number – as it occurs the most times (8). It would be easy to put this kind of information into a bar graph.

## Distribution

The idea of normal distribution is important in statistics. If you are seeking to establish patterns for the occurrence of a particular thing, providing the sample used is big enough (such as trying to establish the usual mid-week bedtime of a group of 30 eighteen-year-olds), and you plot the resulting times from your enquiry onto a line graph, you should end up with a bell-shaped line. This is because one or two of the samples will go to bed much earlier or much later than most of the group with many more going roughly at the same time (see Figure 11.11).

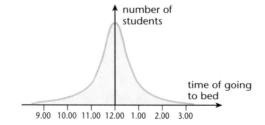

*Figure 11.11*

## Probability

This is defined as 'the numerical estimate of the likelihood of an event occurring', and involves measuring or determining the likelihood that an event or experiment will have a particular outcome. It is the necessary foundation for statistics. For example, a die thrown can have six possible outcomes, each equally likely. The chance of throwing a 5 or 6 is therefore 2/6 (or 1/3).

This concept is used to determine statistically the probability of an outcome that cannot be readily tested, or that is impossible to obtain – for example, if long-range statistics show that out of every 100 people aged between 20 and 30, 42 will be alive at the age of 70, the assumption is that a person between these ages has a 42% probability of surviving until 70.

## Mathematical reasoning

## Formula

| AQA A | M2 |
| AQA B | M3 |
| EDEXCEL | M2 |
| OCR | M2 |

Per cent is the Latin for 'of a hundred'.

### Percentages

A percentage is simply a fraction with 100 as the denominator.

20% means 20/100 (or 1/5).

To express a percentage as a fraction, first write it as a fraction using the denominator 100 and then reduce it to its lowest terms:

e.g. 25% is 25/100 or 5/20 or 1/4
18% is 18/100 or 9/50.

To change a fraction to a percentage multiply it by 100%.

e.g. 1/4 x 100% = 100/4 = 25%
$3^1/_2 = {}^7/_2$ x 100% = 700/2 = 350%.

Worked examples of percentages.

A sale offers 15% off normal prices. If a coat is normally £80, what will be its sale price?

First find 15% of the normal price of £80.
15% = 15/100 = 0.15
15% of £80 = 0.15 x £80 = £12.00
So, the sale price is £80 – £12 = £68.

A student scores 32 marks out of 80 in an exam – what is his percentage score?

32 out of 80 = 32/80
As a percentage this is 32/80 x 100% = 40%.

Worked examples of percentages.

A worker's hours are reduced from 40 to 37 a week – what is the percentage decrease?

Original hours = 40 Decrease = 3
Fractional decrease = 3/40
Percentage decrease = $\frac{3}{40_2} \times \cancel{100}^5 = \frac{15}{2} = 7^1/_2\%$.

### Equations

Equations that use simple letters and numbers are called **linear equations**.

When solving an equation you must do the same thing to both sides of the equation

e.g. $5x = 60$ The inverse of x 5 is ÷ 5, so divide both sides by 5:

$\frac{\cancel{5}x}{\cancel{5}} = \frac{\cancel{60}^{12}}{5}$ so $x = 12$

$3x + 4 = 19$ The inverse of (+4) is (–4), so subtract 4 from both sides:
$3x + 4 – 4 = 19 – 4$ so $3x = 15 x = 5$

$7x = 4x + 9$ Look at which side has fewest $x$s and remove this from both sides
$7x – 4x = 4x – 4x + 9$ so $3x = 9 x = 3$.

The type of maths you will be expected to attempt in a General Studies exam is concerned with mathematical reasoning and the application of number. The extent to which this will involve individual mathematical calculations will vary, depending on which specification you have studied.

The material covered in the sections in this chapter on amounts and sizes, Pythagoras' Theorem, scales and proportions, statistics, graphs and formulae might well come up in a General Studies exam.

If you are studying key skills as part of your General Studies course the different awarding bodies' specifications will enable you to perform at Level 3 in the application of number.

KEY POINT

## Sample question and model answer

This question is a specimen from the OCR General Studies AS Level exam.

The graph below shows the results of an investigation into the variation in dry mass of 100 peas. The total mass of the sample was 27.48 g.

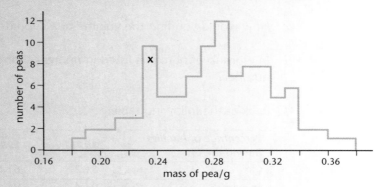

Mean = $\dfrac{27.48}{100}$

Mode = the most common mass.

Remember to provide a key for your chart.

(a) (i) What was the mass of the heaviest pea?
(ii) State the mean mass of the peas
(iii) What was the modal mass of the peas?

(b) Sketch a pie chart of the experimental data showing the percentage of sampled peas with dry masses in the following classes:

• less than 0.24 g
• 0.24 g to less than 0.32 g
• 0.32 g or greater.

*(a) (i) Mass of heaviest pea in range 0.37 – 0.38 g*
*(ii) The mean mass of the peas is 27.48/100 = 0.2748*
*(iii) The modal mass of the peas is 12 entries*

*(b) Circle*

*Dividing from 12 o'clock*
*Angles of 76°, 223°, 61°*
*(remember – the combined angles always = 360°)*
*Key*

*OCR initial AS/A2 Draft General Studies 1998*

## *Practice examination questions*

1   Use Pythagoras' Theorem to find the length of the hypotenuse of a right-angled triangle with a base of 7 cm and right-angle side of 10 cm.

2   How would you find the volume of a cuboid?

3   In a group of numbers listed in numerical order, which would be the median number?

4   Look at the following table:

| Percentage of families having use of: | 1971 | 1981 | 1991 | 1993 |
|---|---|---|---|---|
| Car | 51.2 | 61.8 | 67.6 | 68.6 |
| Television | 91.4 | 96.6 | 98.3 | n/a |
| Central heating | 32.2 | 60.5 | 81.8 | 82.5 |
| Fridge | 68.8 | 96.1 | 99.2 | 99.1 |
| Freezer | n/a | n/a | 83.5 | 86.6 |
| Washing machine | 63.3 | 80.7 | 87.9 | 89.3 |
| Video | n/a | n/a | 69.3 | 73.4 |

(n/a = not available)

(a)  Construct a bar chart showing car ownership in 1971, 1981 and 1991.

(b)  Construct a line graph using all the figures provided to show increasing use of washing machines.

# Practice examination answers

## Chapter 1  Society

1 The methods used would be (ii), (iii), (iv) and (v).

2 An answer could touch on things such as:
- glossy prospectus
- school uniform
- good examination results
- extra-curricular activities
- friends' siblings' stories
- perception/rumour
- newspaper stories
- advertising
- Open Days/evenings
- friendliness of the institution.

3 In attempting this answer the following points are relevant:
- League tables are measures introduced by Parliament.
- They make information available to the public.
- The information applies to schools and colleges.
- The main focus is on exam results in national tests (KS2/KS4).
- Increasingly, other information, such as attendance rates, is included.
- They are published annually.

*Advantages are:*
- Attitudes towards education are changing and availability of information to the public is now considered more important.
- Schools are public bodies and need to be more accountable.
- Information on such matters as examination results and attendance tells schools how they are doing.
- Information can help schools to identify strengths and weaknesses.
- Information can be used to help raise performance.
- Parents can use the information to help choose schools.

*Disadvantages are:*
- League tables concentrate on areas that are easily measurable.
- Schools do many other things which are not in the tables.
- League tables say more about a school's intake of pupils than about what it achieves.
- Schools with a large intake of low ability pupils experience even greater difficulties following the publication of results.

4 Points which could be made in favour of 'wealth creation' creating a fair society include the following.
- Greater wealth leads to more spending, thus increasing purchasing and employment.
- Greater wealth leads to more money being collected by the government – so there is more money to spend on health, education, etc.
- Better to increase global wealth to increase the money available for better services;
- People feel motivated by the thought that they can play a part in making themselves better off.
- 'Fair' does not always mean 'all the same' – no truly equal society has ever existed and those who can create wealth should be encouraged.
- The 'trickle-down' theory of economics (where the money of the rich gradually trickles down and creates work for others in providing for the needs of the rich).

Points against the idea that wealth creation is not the best way to create a fair society are as follows.
- A concentration of wealth in comparatively few hands fosters inequality.
- If wealth creation becomes the most important social and political goal it is easy to forget the poor and underprivileged.
- A society dedicated to making wealth is not 'fair'.
- The trickle-down theory did not appear to work in the 1980s in the USA/UK in spite of the support of Reagan/Thatcher (e.g. riots in areas of the UK during the 1980s).
- Wealth creation exacerbates the 'them and us' syndrome.

## Chapter 2  Political concepts

1 (c) A system of ideas which underlies social or political action.

2 (a), (c) and (d).

3 (c) first past the post.

4 (d) parliament.

5 *Arguments for:*
- It is such an important part of the political process that everyone of voting age should do so. (Other countries, such as Australia, impose fines if people do not vote.)
- Not voting is an insult to all the people who have died in the comparatively recent past in order to secure the right to vote (e.g. the Chartists – John Frost and the March on Newport 1839; the Suffragettes - Emily Davidson throwing herself under the King's horse at the Derby in 1913).

*Arguments against:*
- If people have no interest in the political system, why should they vote? – Is it their fault or the system's?
- If voting is made compulsory it would encourage spoilt papers and 'silly' candidates, or, more seriously, extremist parties and candidates;
- If voting is done in secret, no one can know what or how people have voted, so why make it compulsory?
- Under the present system, people who have not voted do not really have any right to complain if they do not like what the party in power is doing; the answer is obvious: use your vote next time.

## Chapter 3  Business concepts

1 *Your answers should cover the following points:*
- The national minimum wage was set by Parliament from 1 April, 1999; (a wage level of £3.60 per hour for those over 21; £3.00 per hour for those aged 18–21); It is an attempt to ensure that certain workers are not exploited by the payment of very low wages.

It is needed in order to:
- bring the UK in line with countries like the USA and some in Europe which already have a minimum wage
- reduce the poverty of those on very low wages
- give additional protection to those who do not, for whatever reason, have any other body to protect their interests.

2 (b) – Black (Caribbean; African and other black people of non-mixed race).

3 *Your answer should cover the following points:*
- Differences between what different people are paid may be historical.
- Pay rates may be based on skills and training.
- Scarcity often helps to determine pay rates.
- Working out what each job is 'worth' is very difficult.
- It might be possible to evaluate what a job is worth by trying to measure output/performance.
- Money is important in terms of helping to motivate people.
- Money is not the only factor – others might include job satisfaction, working conditions, proximity to home, and so on.

**4** *Your answer should cover the following points:*
*For the banning of strikes in the public sector:*
- Strikes hold the broader society to ransom.
- Strikes hurt many people who are not remotely involved in the dispute.
- Strikes can damage the whole national economy (e.g. strikes on the railway, in ports, etc.).
- Strikes can lead to potentially dangerous situations (e.g. strikes by fire-fighters).
- Strikes are far more than an action against a single employer – there is an intention of causing widespread disruption.
- Strikes are open to political manipulation by extremists seeking to disrupt society.
- Public sector workers have a duty to the public.

*Against the banning of strikes in the public sector:*
- The freedom to withdraw one's labour is a basic principle of a free society.
- Strikes are a valid tool for people who have been in traditionally low-paid/low-status jobs serving the public.
- Opposition to such strikes is often whipped up by the right-wing press who highlight and magnify 'worst case' situations.
- Taking away the right to strike would leave many public sector employees powerless and often in comparative poverty.
- A ban could be seen as an act of repression by the government which could be 'the thin end of the wedge', eventually spreading to other groups.

## Chapter 4  Culture and aesthetics

**1** You could have said any three of the following: Wales, Northern Ireland, Cornwall, Isle of Man.

**2** 'Romeo and Juliet', and 'West Side Story'.

**3** Music.

**4** The introduction should include a definition of multi-cultural Britain. The essay then takes two distinct parts:

*Challenges* – these should describe racism as demonstrated through:
- attacks on people from ethnic minorities
- individuals and families subject to attacks
- murder of black people – most recently, Stephen Lawrence
- higher levels of arrests and searches of black people by the police
- racist chants at soccer matches
- creation of areas of social inequality in some towns, etc.

*Opportunities* – these should include:
- the chance to broaden our horizons by finding out about other cultures and communities
- the fact that the numbers of people travelling to and from areas such as the West Indies, or the south Asian sub-continent makes travel to such areas relatively cheap and frequent
- we can listen to music, see pieces of art or read literature from around the world more easily since they have a ready market in the UK
- restaurants, cafés and other places selling food and drink from around the world have opened and have become popular
- we can experience a wide range of religious traditions.

*The conclusion should:* seek to establish a balance between challenges and opportunities and suggest ways you can think of to develop positive multi-cultural experience.

## Chapter 5  Beliefs, values and morals

**1** In state schools:
- Religious education is a compulsory subject.
- There has to be a daily act of collective worship.
- Every local authority must publish an approved syllabus for religious education.

In the 19th century, the churches were the major provider of schools in Britain.
- Today there are 4,700 Anglican (Church of England and Church in Wales) schools and 2,500 Roman Catholic schools.

**2** The three main groups are:
- The Orthodox church.
- The Roman Catholic church.
- The Protestant churches (or 'Free churches').

**3** These are a form of shorthand, reflecting differing kinds of importance given to the rights and authority of the individual. 'Right wing' means a greater importance is laid on the individual, left-wing means a greater importance is given to the community and to collective duties and responsibilities.

**4** Your answer will need to acknowledge that, while many people do not hold any religious views themselves, much that underlies the values of society has its origins in religious practice and values. Points that should be made include the following:
- Since human beings are essentially moral beings they are likely to develop values that would support and promote effective communities – 'Love your neighbour as yourself' is not only a God-given law, but simply reflects a positive way of living. Since most people looked to a deity to provide an explanation for things in a pre-scientific age, such social values were actually assigned to a divine origin.
- Britain has seen a decline in Christian observance over the last fifty years – particularly in the Church of England, which for many is the religion of the 'status quo'. Nonetheless, it is still the case that Christian values underpin many of the institutions in British society today. Parliament and most local councils begin their meetings with prayers, and the Church of England has (since its sixteenth-century break from the Roman Catholic church) had senior bishops in the House of Lords as a matter of right – although proposals to abolish the Lords in its present format could change this.
- Social values – a belief in 'providing for the needy' – can also be said to be based on the teachings found not only in the Bible, but also in other holy books.
- Many people who claim there has been a decline in social values will ascribe this to a decline in doing what is 'right' as defined by religious tradition.
- One problem for those who support the idea that religious values lie at the heart of all other value systems is that there is no single set of religious values, even within the same religion. Some Christians are radical socialists, others traditional conservatives, but all will claim that they follow religious values in their particular lifestyle.

Your conclusions will, to some extent, depend on whether or not you believe in a God. However, whichever side you belong to, take care to be objective in your arguments, although you can come to a personal conclusion having looked at both sides of the picture objectively.

## Chapter 6  Creativity and innovation

*1* The main technological advances were:
- steel-framed buildings which meant that walls were no longer responsible for carrying the whole weight of a building. This meant that:
  - buildings could go much higher
  - walls could be decorative.
- the invention of the passenger lift (elevator) which meant that taller buildings were a practical possibility – people didn't have to go up many flights of stairs to access the top floors
- reinforced concrete became popular as a flexible tool for filling the space between the steel frames.

*2* • George Orwell was seeking to describe his view of the Soviet Union and how it was not proving true to its revolutionary origins.
- He used animals because he was writing an allegory – conveying a message through the telling of a story that appears to be about something else. Since Orwell was writing in the years immediately after the end of World War II during which the Soviet Union had been our war-time friend and ally, he had to put his essentially critical message across in this way.

*3* • The Musical has been popular since the 1920s – from then until the 1950s life was very hard for many people, with high unemployment, followed by a world war. Musicals tended therefore to be escapist and glamorous – with lavish sets and troupes of dancing girls.
- By the 1960s and the time of the 'pop revolution' life was very different – many people were affluent, few were unemployed and people tended to be optimistic. Serious, even sombre, themes began to be tackled in musicals (such as the Vietnam War in the musical 'Hair').
- In more recent years there has tended to be a reversion to the earlier, more escapist style in musicals. It can be argued that this reversion to a more escapist style is at least in part due to increased unemployment and

insecurity in the 1980s. However, the Musical as an art form has gained popularity again in the UK in large part because of the emergence of a new generation of composers like Andrew Lloyd-Webber. Political themes are still tackled (for example, Victor Hugo's story, 'Les Miserables').

*4* A short introduction should set out the types of buildings you are going to discuss, e.g. housing; shops; churches, etc. Since the question asks for specific examples, ensure that you provide these. The points you make could cover the following:
- How would various different types of housing affect things such as a sense of neighbourhood and community, of pride and belonging, or on the other hand of isolation and a potential unhappiness? (types of housing could include a cottage in a rural village, traditional terraces in industrial towns, a council estate in a large city or high-rise town blocks).
- Do we all have equal access to all kinds of shops? How might you feel if you went shopping at Harrods instead of your local town shops? What effects do large, airy, out-of-town shopping complexes have on our patterns of spending and lifestyle? (Types of shops you could mention include: small local shops on street corners; local shopping centres, many of which are shuttered at night; brightly lit shops with pop music playing found in new shopping developments.)
- How do churches reflect the divisions in society – the C of E on the whole for the upper and middle classes, the Roman Catholic church or the Non-conformist chapel for the working classes. In modern church design buildings are often much lighter and arranged in a circle, or semi-circle so there is no social hierarchy, etc.
- Remember to provide a good range of buildings to support the points you make, otherwise you won't have answered the question properly and will lose marks.

## Chapter 7  Media and communication

*1* Answers should include the following points:
- smaller in size, easy to carry and read
- stories and articles are brief and can be read quickly – maybe little and often in a crowded day for the reader
- concentration on 'human interest' stories and celebrities
- dominating photographic images on the front pages
- headlines are eye-catching, often in the form of a pun
- layout follows a regular routine pattern – readers know where to look for the different features
- often very nationalistic in tone and content, especially in sports' coverage.

*2* You might consider such occasions as:
- in times of war (e.g. the Falklands and the Gulf Wars) the Ministry of Defence might regulate information to the press so that:
  - morale remains high at home and public support for the war is sustained
  - the enemy is not given details they could use to their advantage
- when obscenity, sexual exploitation, or other things that could outrage or inflame public opinion might be published. (A classic example of censorship being imposed came in the late 1960s when *Oz* magazine had to remove a poem about Jesus Christ after Mary Whitehouse brought a successful prosecution under the blasphemy laws, which are still in effect in the UK.)
- when the private lives of individuals (even ones frequently in the news) are invaded to the extent that their rights become infringed in a massive way – going beyond a 'public right to know'.

NB Candidates might well be expected to back up such points with actual examples – always look to provide supporting evidence to gain the highest marks.

*3* Try to give examples from different soap operas to show:
- the number of exciting events that occur in daily life are exaggerated (especially in order to lead to a climax in every episode of some soaps) – life is actually far more mundane for most people
- the whole of humanity cannot be reflected in a tableau that is geographically very compact – Ramsey Street, Coronation Street and Albert Square, for example
- a lot of the action takes place in one or two focused spots, such as The Queen Vic or The Rovers Return pubs, rather than in the community as a whole
- some Soaps, especially Australian imports, concentrate on projecting an overwhelmingly young and glamorous image with little harsh social reality ever seen.

You may well find other valid points to put down. Examiners will give you credit for them if they can be justified, even if they don't appear in the Exam Board's formal mark scheme.

*4* Your answer should consider the balance between the rights of the individual, the right of the community to know what is going on and the right of the Press to publish in an unfettered way in a democracy. You should tackle questions such as:
- Should we have a 'freedom of the individual' law as many democracies do – the individual also has freedoms, as well as society?
- Do newspapers go beyond the bounds of

'reasonableness' in seeking stories or photographs of people – gantries erected outside their homes to get photographs, or the 'paparazzi' pursuing figures like Diana, Princess of Wales, to the point of possibly contributing to her death by chasing her car?

- Does everyone have rights to freedom and privacy?
- Do editors abuse their freedoms within our democracy – perhaps running the risk that eventually those freedoms might be limited for everybody?
- Where such stories are only published as a way of increasing circulation how can any lofty high moral ground be argued by the newspaper concerned?

A strong case can be advanced for limiting the power of newspapers. However, on the other hand:

- Surely the public have a right to expect its leaders to be above reproach, and we have a right to know when they fail to act accordingly. Indeed, some would agree that the press has a duty to inform us about our leaders' behaviour – if this was not possible we would risk becoming a Totalitarian society where leaders could not be challenged.
- Privacy laws might protect those who are rich and privileged, allowing them to do things that the majority would not find acceptable.
- Since the royal family is often featured as the model for the family and are supported by millions of pounds of public funds, so we should know about their lives in detail.
- Many articles actually appear as public relations stories issued by the PR agents for the rich and famous who want and need to remain in the public eye.
- There are already the general laws of slander and libel which act as effective limits on the power of the Press to publish stores that are not true.

## Chapter 8  The nature of science

1  'Inductive' means what can be induced – i.e. has a conclusion that goes beyond what can be definitely proved and which will be a definite outcome.

2  A 'hypothesis' is an idea that seeks to explain a collection of known facts and is a starting point for further work. A 'law' is a generalised, or universal formulation based on a series of events or processes observed to recur regularly under certain conditions – or, more simply, universal patterns in native/universal generalisations.

3  Classification is a way of bringing methodology and order to a situation. For example, the great Swedish biologist Linnaeus published his classification of plants and animals using two Latin names for each species as early as 1749 and this has remained a model ever since.

4  Your answer should cover the following points:
- Darwin was the first European to put forward this scientific theory that was so much at odds with the prevailing religious view of the time (as set out in the opening paragraphs of the book of Genesis – that there is a God, who created the Earth and in six days inhabited it with all plants and animals, culminating in people, who were created in the image of God). Science had devised a theory that matched what could be observed with this religious view – the 'Catastrophe Theory'. According to this the earth had experienced a series of creations of plant and animal life, all of which (except the last) had been destroyed by catastrophe – the most recent of which was the Flood, from which only those plants and creatures on board Noah's Ark had been saved.
- The background to Darwin's work was his work on the Galapagos Islands while travelling round the world aboard *The Beagle* in particular. His great book *On the Origin of Species* was eagerly awaited – it completely sold out on the first day it was published in 1859.
- Some scientists (usually those with strong Christian beliefs) rejected the Darwinian theory of natural selection (later described as 'the survival of the fittest') saying that it would never be more than a hypothesis, because it could not be experimentally tested. However, many scientists accepted Darwin's claims – it was the Christian church that created the huge outcry.
- Many church members objected to Darwin's theory because:
  - it suggested that the Bible might not be literal truth
  - it suggested that God did not directly create each species at a specific time, but rather that there was a natural development, largely in response to the environment
  - humans had evolved from other species rather than being specially created to share eternity with God.
- This is an 'abiding controversy' – for example, in some areas in the USA a minority of the community were able to force through a referendum to ban the teaching of evolution in schools, and to replace this with the Creationist view.
- The Christian church has, to a very large degree, come to accept a Darwinian view of evolution, which has ended the controversy for all except a small minority.

## Chapter 9  Morality and science

1  Satellites have enabled:
- global communications systems
- live TV and radio broadcasts from around the world
- TV channels being received from satellite, not from terrestrial links
- the spread of mass education through distance-learning techniques in remote parts of the world
- a far greater understanding of weather patterns and systems – severe weather is a major threat in some areas
- hi-tech surveillance of military capability – the 'spy in the sky' – makes it less easy for the military build-up that might threaten stability to take place.

2  Dangers of nuclear-power generation include:
- high levels of radioactivity in various stages of the process
- the need to store increasing amounts of highly radioactive material for thousands of years when the necessary technology and storage facilities have not yet been fully developed (e.g. there is still no permanent storage facility in the UK)
- risks in the transit of nuclear material to and from power stations – although the nuclear industry claims that the flasks that are used are impregnable
- enriched uranium created in the generating process has potential use in making nuclear weapons and could fall into the hands of potential enemies of the state
- any leakage of radiation from a power station has the potential for a major catastrophe – Chernobyl being perhaps the best-known example to date.

3  Think of different areas of domestic entertainment – radio, music, TV and video are perhaps the most common.
- Radio – Early sets were very large, because they needed large valves. These were replaced by transistors, which miniaturised the size of radio. The development of battery-operated radios enabled them to be portable. Radios as

part of music centres started in combination with a record player, and, again, this was large – a piece of household furniture. Today, radio is a part of music centres, the smallest of which can be battery operated and are easily portable.

- CDs – The forerunners of CDs and records started in the nineteenth century as cylinders with power from a 'wind-up handle'. Records then developed – these were easily broken, 78-revolutions-per-minute (RPM) disks played on record players that had big metal 'trumpet speakers'. In the 1950s records began to be made of vinyl plastic – single songs on disks that played at 45 revolutions per minute, while LPs (long-playing records) turned at 33 revolutions per minute. During the 1970s audio-cassettes became increasingly popular as they did not scratch – a problem which easily distorted the sound quality of vinyl records. In the 1980s and 90s compact disks became increasingly popular, virtually eliminating the use of vinyl disks. CDs use laser technology and have the advantage that sound quality is better and cannot be distorted.
- Television – Experimental programmes were broadcast just before the war, but a national service operated by the BBC was delayed by the hostilities. Until the 1960s, programmes were broadcast in black and white only. From the 1960s colour programmes were introduced, and picture quality improved when the number of lines (which combine to create the impression of a single picture) was increased to 625 for every screen image. Contemporary developments have seen cable and satellite broadcasts – the latter having a revolutionary effect. Digital technology has also seen a major improvement in the quality of sound and picture.
- Video – Recent developments enable us to watch feature films that we have recorded on video tape, as well as

enabling programmes to be *recorded and sorted*. 'Camcorders' are cameras that enable people to make their very own videos – these have virtually replaced the old 16mm home-movie cameras that were popular between the 1950s and 1970s.

**4** *Arguments in favour of genetically modified foods include:*
- they will enable a large increase in production – needed to help feed the world's growing population
- resistance to pests and diseases built into GM foods will reduce the need for chemical sprays
- varieties of crops will be developed for areas where it is not possible to grow crops at the moment – thus helping to sustain local communities in areas of the world where life is often a struggle at present. Many who oppose GM foods are wealthy residents of the wealthy world who have the luxury of choice – GM foods could help transform the lives of the poor.

*Arguments against GM foods include:*
- farmers will create huge areas of a single crop where no other plants will grow, thus destroying eco-systems and putting many species under threat
- GM food might create new illnesses to which there is no known cure – we could be poisoning ourselves
- there have not been enough laboratory experiments to test for longer-term effects – we are 'human guinea pigs' for scientists and technologists
- development has been dominated by large multinational firms like Monsanto who are primarily interested in commercial success, not humanitarian motives. Control needs to be taken by government scientists for greater objectivity.

## Chapter 10  Science and culture

**1** **Science** can be defined as 'the branch of knowledge conducted on objective principles involving systematised observation of, and experiment with, phenomena, especially those concerned with the material and the functions of the physical universe.' **Ideology** can be defined as 'the system of ideas that lies at the heart of an economic or political theory at the macro level, or the manner of thinking of a social class or individual.'

**2** Gene therapy is the process of changing the inherited characteristics of an organism through altering elements of its genetic material. There are human illnesses that are caused by faulty genes, many have passed down through generations within a family. If therapy can alter the gene that causes the problem the illness will not occur – a good example of this is Huntington's Chorea: a crippling brain disease that strikes in early middle age. It is estimated that the gene that leads to this illness is carried by around 10,000 people in Britain and it could soon be eradicated as a result of gene therapy.

**3** Some people see abortion (or 'termination') as a simple medical process, that, particularly in the early stages of pregnancy, is in effect the removal of an integral part of the woman's own body. However, other people, particularly those with religious views, believe that life starts at the moment of conception and that the bundle of cells that multiply to become a foetus and then a child still represents life – and that to end its existence is therefore tantamount to murder. Some people who hold this view have formed themselves into a variety of sometimes quite radical groups committed to direct action, whose sole aim is what they describe as 'the protection of the unborn child'. In the UK the charity LIFE is perhaps the best-known such group, although it pursues its campaign within the confines of the law. Many of its members and much of its funding comes from members of the Roman Catholic church. There is also

the theological argument that it is God who creates life – and that to interfere with this is to assume a power beyond that intended for humans.

**4** In order to get good marks in the exam you will not only have to give a simple description of the life and work of your chosen example but make sure to provide analysis of this person's contribution to enhancing our lives. An outline, using the example of the life and work of Albert Einstein, might cover the following points:
- Albert Einstein, 1879–1955, radically revised the ideas of classical physics with his theories of relativity. During the 1940s the work he had done in explaining the relationship between protons and neutrons and their separation was crucial in the work leading to the development and use of the atomic bomb (though Einstein was known around the world as a pacifist).
- Einstein was not always seen as leading opinion in his scientific beliefs – for example, he refused to follow mainstream efforts in developing quantum theory, saying in *The Observer* in 1954 'I cannot believe that God plays dice with the cosmos'.
- In 1905 Einstein published the theory of relativity, with its central notion that space and time have to be considered as uniform and not as two separate things – which changed the prevailing view of space based on the seventeenth-century ideas of Newton. In 1916 Einstein published his General Theory of Relativity. This theory explained, for example, variations in the orbital motion of planets, and predicted the bending of starlight in the vicinity of a massive body such as the sun.
- When the theory was confirmed by experiment in 1919 Einstein achieved worldwide fame. In 1921 he was awarded the Nobel Prize for physics. He became seen as a world citizen, and he used his fame quite deliberately to further his own political and social views, especially on pacifism and the creation of a Jewish state.

- In 1939 he was one of a group of scientists who wrote to President Roosevelt warning him of the possibility of the atomic bomb, and of likely work on its development by German scientists. However, he played no direct part in the subsequent research that culminated in the bomb being exploded over Hiroshima and Nagasaki at the end of World War II.
- After the war Einstein remained a prominent figure in the campaign for disarmament and for world government.

When the State of Israel was created he was offered the Presidency, but turned it down.
- Even Einstein's social theories were worked out with scientific methodology. Right until his death he felt that his science was the most important thing in his life – he said that of everything he had done, his work on discovering the nature of the universe would have lasting meaning.

## Chapter 11  *Mathematical reasoning and its application*

**1** Hypotenuse$^2$ = $7^2$ + $10^2$
∴ h$^2$ = 49 + 100
∴ h = $\sqrt{149}$
= 12.2

**2** Length x breadth x height

**3** The number that is the middle value of the group of values (numbers) provided.

**4** (a)

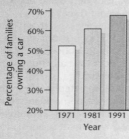

(b)

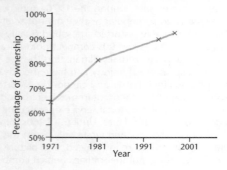

# Index